It's the 1950s

It's the 1950s

Let's Pretend We're Happy

JUDITH FORSYTHE

It's the 1950s: Let's Pretend We're Happy

A True Story Of Rebelling Against Feminine Roles
Of The 1950's And Finding Freedom

Published by:
Judith Forsythe

ISBN: 978-0615945538

For our families:
Those to whom Fate conveys us
And those to whom we give ourselves

Acknowledgements

My thanks to the librarians of the Marshall Public Library and the volunteers of the Clark County Genealogical Society for their cheerful support and assistance. I couldn't have done it without you.

To say thank you is insufficient, but I must extend heartfelt appreciation to my husband for keeping the cogs of life greased and spinning.

Table of Contents

1

It's the 1950s: Let's Pretend We're Happy

IN THE AUTUMN of 1951 when I was seven, Dad moved our family – my mother, myself and my two brothers, David, then five, and Brad, three years old – to Marshall, Illinois, where most of his relatives lived. I have no idea how Dad was able to convince my mother, a Chicago born and bred city girl, to move to Marshall with its dangerous livestock; trees for her children to fall out of; a lake for them to drown in; and berries, fruits, and vegetables that didn't grow on clearly-labeled shelves at the grocery store. And, if those features weren't sufficiently alarming, she also found herself lodged in the bull's-eye of her husband's expansive family circle but two hundred miles from her own family, specifically the bulwark of her mother.

Marshall did not slavishly copy Chicago's street grid pattern, presenting homes on identical squares of greenery and in precise lines like cadets on parade. Marshall's houses, individualistic in style but tending to farmhouse, staggered up and down the streets on lots of varying sizes and shapes. This resulted in even next-door neighbors not standing wall to wall in symmetrical lines, and certainly not as in Chicago where next-door often means shoulder-to-shoulder or even like conjoined twins with a common wall. Dad installed us in what was always known as the old Montgomery house at 310 North Second Street. Our immediate neighbor to the north was Dad's paternal grandfather, named Benjamin but commonly known as Pop, who lived there with his second wife Edith and her two sons from a prior relationship. Pop's first wife Ruth Ettie, née Laufman, or Mom, whom I vaguely remember as a short plump woman with waves of white hair pulled into a loose bun, had died in a 1949 plane crash along with her youngest daughter Martha Jane and Jane's husband. Nearly half an acre of grassland and one of the ubiquitous drainage ditches of southern Illinois separated our house from that of Pop and Edith.

Dad's parents (Ora Benjamin, known to his contemporaries as O.B., and Florence Louise, née Parks) whom we called Pappy and Gramma, lived five houses south of us at 204 North Second Street. Dad's maternal grandmother Alice Mae, née Ward who was nicknamed Bomma lived with them. We quickly made the acquaintance of the line of neighbors between our new home and that of Pappy and Gramma. In a southerly direction they were the McNairy's, an elderly couple with a granddaughter my age; Aunt Bertha Kannemacher, not my aunt but that of my soon to be best friend Karen who lived across the street from Pappy and Gramma; Adie Thornburgh, a blind elderly widow who lived alone as did Aunt Bertha; and a young couple with two or three children but no telephone. If the need arose, the exceptionally timorous mother sent the oldest daughter to Karen or Gramma's house to request that they place the phone call for her. I seldom saw this woman; I don't believe I ever heard her speak.

Soon after moving into the old Montgomery house, my brothers and I discovered a cache of coal-like lumps in the sheltered corner where Dad's workshop joined the back porch and under the two steps jerry-rigged from bricks and a slab of sandstone which descended to the lawn on the north side of our new home. But unlike dusty opaque coal, these objects were smooth to the touch and a translucent dark yellow. What looked to our innocent eyes like a mosquito was imprisoned within one of these lumps. It's a testament to our inquisitiveness about our new environment that we had rooted out this mysterious golden horde because it had been covered over with layers of leaves blown into that nook over who knows how many recurring seasons.

Pappy explained to us that our newfound treasure was amber, a fossilized resin produced by extinct coniferous trees, pieces of which often contain, as ours did, the bodies of trapped insects. I have no idea what became of our amber. One thing I do know, however, is that our seven years in Marshall have become like that insect but enrobed in not-to-be-trusted memory rather than immutable amber.

The fifties in retrospect seem to be less a decade and more an era concurrent with the presidency of Dwight D. Eisenhower from 1953 to 1961. Those years were an aberration. The convergence of events from which they resulted does not seem likely to be repeated. No World War II battles were fought on United States soil, so our country escaped the ruin suffered by other combatants. The young males returning from the battle front no longer needed to save up money or establish themselves before taking a wife and starting a family because they were rewarded with sweet deals on home mortgages and school loans underwritten by our government. The sudden need for pre-fab housing outside central cities, appliances and furniture to provision those houses, manufacturing plants to churn out those goods, and highways to connect as well as cars to transport newlyweds to homes now distant from job sources created employment for our speedily demobilized armed service returnees. Medical facilities and schools also sprang up to accommodate the post war pregnancy epidemic. They too had to be built, staffed, and provisioned.

One bleak November day during the early fifties, we drove from Marshall to central Illinois to visit the family of my father's older brother who lived in one of the conventional landscapes of fifties suburbia on the outskirts of Champaign. Their house was a shoebox on a cement slab. It had the requisite front room picture window. Their front yard was a pathetic patch of frozen mud and frostbitten grass with one spindly excuse of a tree. Their back yard was identical to the front minus the tree. Not only was there nothing to do or see at their house, but there were also miles of the same dreary vista. My cousins, Sue, two years older than me, and Butch, approximately my age, didn't seem to be aware of the sterility of their environment.

They were extremely well-behaved and not allowed to argue with each other or raise their voices in the house or ask their parents for anything a second time if it was denied on their first request. Like many other children with whom I was acquainted at that time, Sue and Butch were required to address their parents as Sir and Ma'am. My uncle was a career army officer and had served on the European front during the Second World War. It seemed like many men of his age and background wanted to carry the hierarchy and discipline they had enjoyed in the military over into their civilian family circles.

That day was a sample of fifties family life that I had the miraculous good fortune to escape because we lived in Marshall. Marshall was a place vastly different than the trackless wasteland of suburbia where the families of television's sitcoms, as well as many real families, resided. My brothers and I weren't confined to a four-room pre-fab house with a picture window on a miniscule treeless lot situated within miles of similarly sterile cookie cutter dwellings and lawns. Our grandparents, great-grandparents, and other close relatives didn't live over the river and through the woods or far, far away. They were next door and up the street, and, unlike suburbs, Marshall had sidewalks so that we could walk or ride our bikes over to see them, as well as everyone and everything else nearby. That also meant that neither our mother nor we were confined in a husbandless, fatherless, ghetto during the day. Nor were we dependent upon someone with a car simply to get to the family doctor's office, dime store or movie theater.

Like all memories, I'm fairly certain that past times are mentally recreated more than recalled. That our reminiscences lack completeness and certainty is, I suspect, what allows many, especially men, to look back on the fifties with baseless fondness. I experienced that time and place as a child, with all the limitations of a naïve young child's perceptions and restrained by the insularity of life in a southern Illinois farm community. My recollections may feel to me like literal snapshots, but I'm cognizant they may be flawed reconstructions. Rather than a fixed fragment of information, each memory may be reconstructed every time I recall it. Components of my memories may be reassembling themselves within the vessel of my current feelings and knowledge into which I pour them. Probably that insect confined in its amber penitentiary, which my siblings and I discovered now sixty years removed, was more static than my life in Marshall is in my memory.

My mother or my brother David, if they recounted the 1950s in Marshall, would offer up a different narrative. In fact, David does remember incidents and individuals differently than I remember them or recalls what I do not. I must concede, as did Wendell Berry in his 1989 book *The Hidden Wound* that, "…I am aware that the truth I am telling may be a very personal one" and "… I write with the feeling that the truth I may tell will not be definitive or objective or even demonstrable…"[1]. Nonetheless, I must bear witness, as only I can, to the life I experienced in that place and time, and with the intent of explicating some of the elements of what has been irrevocably eradicated by the forward rush of time.

---

1. Wendell Berry, *The Hidden Wound* (San Francisco: Northpoint Press, 1989) 48.

2

Welcome to Marshall (Population 2,960) "where the highways cross and the porch lights burn all night"

THAT MESSAGE WAS borne by signs posted on the major roads leading into Marshall. It was the town's motto and every word of it was true. Marshall, afloat on the subtly undulating terrain of the eastern niche of southern Illinois, is situated near the Illinois–Indiana border on Route 1 just off its juncture with Interstate Highway 70. Terre Haute, Indiana, seventeen miles east on Interstate 70, is the closest large city. Chicago is a distant 198 miles north via Route 1 and Interstate 57 – and a lifetime removed in lived experience.

Seat of Clark County and business center of the surrounding agricultural community, the town's commercial core was strung out along its one main street, Archer Avenue, and clustered around the Clark County Courthouse Square. Known as Marshall's uptown, it was comprised of a constellation of pool halls; bars; fraternal organizations such as the Elks, Moose and VFW lodge; two restaurants;

the drug store (individually owned, not a Walgreens nor a CVS); and the one-room library on the second floor of an Archer Avenue storefront. Archer Avenue, named after William B. Archer who organized Marshall in 1835, carries that name only within Marshall's boundaries. Elsewhere it is the National Road, the first federally-funded road in U.S. history, built between 1811 and 1834. In many places, it is also known as Route 40 or as the Cumberland Road because it originated in Cumberland, Maryland. The National Road reached Illinois in 1830. So integral is the National Road to the Marshall area that The Welcome Center at Harlan Hall (built in 1872) maintains a permanent exhibit of dioramas relating the story of its political backers, surveyors, and builders.

Like the ripples generated by a stone flung into the unnamed lake at the extreme edge of our property, one-of-a-kind single-family homes surrounded Marshall's center and radiated outward to the town's perimeter. The little town's third ring of concentric circles was given over to family farms. Here you would find the farmhouses, enlarged by accretion, now surrendering their exterior paint and right angles to the forces of entropy; farmyards flecked with white Leghorn hens; weary billboard barns, and twisted wire and wood slat corn-cribs losing their struggle with gravity's unrelenting drag alongside the always newer-looking silvery grain silos; acres of corn and soybean fields progressing, through the May to October growing season, from vibrant green to striated sorrel. Here also were the mucky pastures populated mostly by white-faced Herefords and the occasional black Aberdeen-Angus that resembled ponderous black boxcars improbably set on four short pegs, as well as herds of Chester White, Berkshire, Poland China and Duroc sows and piglets.

My father's ancestors, William and Esther Forsythe, moved to the area sometime in 1826, nine years before Marshall was founded. The town was named, as are many other cities and counties, for Chief Justice of the Supreme Court John Marshall (1801-35). In 1832 the death of one of William and Esther's sons occasioned the opening of the Forsythe Cemetery, which even today remains embedded in the cornfields five miles north of Marshall along Route 1. From William and Esther's arrival in 1826 through the fifties when I lived there unto the present day, that area was, and still is, seeded with Forsythes. I have already noted my paternal great-grandparents and grandparents. My father was in business with his Uncle Lauf, who with his wife Mary and their two daughters, Kay and Valerie, and son Jackie, lived a few blocks across town from us. Dad's Uncle Glen Arthur who was always called big Bill (as opposed to my father who was little Bill) and Aunt Dorothy with their two children owned a farm a short distance from town. Those are just the family members whom I remember living in closest proximity to us, but we were related to every Forsythe in and around Marshall.

So it can't be said that my family was unknown in the area. But throughout our entire 1951–1958 sojourn in Marshall, the house my father bought and rehabbed for us was known as the old Montgomery house. A late 1940s Marshall telephone directory identifies one Ralph Montgomery as living at that address. The September 21, 1980, Terre Haute *Tribune-Star* provides the death notice for Mr. Montgomery. He died at the age of eighty in Union Hospital in Terre Haute. The obituary doesn't state where he had been living although his surviving daughter was listed as a Marshall resident. I'm in the dark as to where and why he or his family moved from their house on North Second Street. The Montgomery family remains a shadowy presence of that place and time, their surname memorialized by a house.

The old Montgomery house was on North Second Street, the last street and line of houses on Marshall's western border. A North First Street did exist but only as a start and stop, dog's hind leg kind of street that did not extend itself behind our own or our closest neighbors' houses. Our home was a hundred year old, two-story, white house with a dull gray tin roof and a façade dominated by a full-width classical columned veranda, front windows symmetrically balanced with a center front door that was flanked by narrow sidelight windows. It was situated on approximately fourteen acres of largely uncultivated land.

As my brothers and I were herded to our beds in the evening, we performed the second half of Marshall's town motto: the daily twilight ritual of turning on the porch light and locking our front door. Our porch light and those of our neighbors and relatives all up and down the narrow anfractuous streets of Marshall burned throughout the night until extinguished the following morning by the earliest rising member of each family. In our case that would have been my father who, when he left for work, also unlocked the door which remained unlocked until that day's end.

My acquaintances today can understand unlocked doors as a relic from a supposedly simpler, safer, more innocent era. But the porch lights burning all night? "Why?" they want to know. I'm stumped. I have no idea because it never occurred to me to ask. Perhaps, it was done because streetlights were few and far between in the residential area circling Marshall's business district and Archer Avenue. Perhaps, we turned on the porch light every night because my father's parents had done so when he was growing up in Marshall, as had their parents before them in an ongoing self-perpetuating ritual. For whatever reason, I spent those years engaging in this unquestioned ceremony peculiar to my life in Marshall in the fifties.

3

The Old Montgomery House

WE LIVED IN the Old Montgomery House. Despite the seven years we resided in, rehabbed, and refashioned that house, it never became the new, the old, or even little Bill Forsythe's house. In the minds and conversations of Marshall's residents, it retained its designation as the old Montgomery House. For $5,000 from the GI Bill, my father acquired not only the house and the fourteen acres on which it sat but also a barn, corn-crib, pig shed, brooder house constructed over a root cellar with its separate batten door, a hen house, an unused two-story building soon razed, and a pint-sized work shop abutting the sizeable, two-level back porch. As my mother tartly observed, "Then we paid another $5,000 to make it habitable."

I didn't realize when we moved into it that the old Montgomery house was an exemplar of the Greek revival farmhouse. The term farmhouse doesn't apply to a style but to its purpose. It gained that appellation because it was located on agricultural land and designed to function for a farming lifestyle. Most likely it was owner-built and its key elements were simplicity and functionality. Like the Montgomery house, many were built with utilitarian porches that were transitional spaces between the very real earth,

23

manure and fodder of the farm and the cleaner wood and fabric inside the house. These houses were also constructed with formal and informal spaces. That explained the parlors and sitting rooms in the front, or formal area, of the house while the kitchen was in the back. Although our house didn't share that particular feature, stairs to upstairs bedrooms were often placed in the back of the house as well.

The Greek revival elements of the old Montgomery house were its portico of tall columns and the horizontal transom over the front door. I thought the house resembled the Tara and Twelve Oaks plantations as they were represented in what was then my favorite movie, *Gone with the Wind*. The old Montgomery house had the same style first floor height veranda spanning the width of its white two-story façade. One of my father's first remodeling projects was to pull off that porch to replace it with a single-step cement stoop, totally out of proportion to the building it fronted, and a walkway attaching the house to the public sidewalk of North Second Street. He covered over the white wood of the exterior with sheets of somber vinyl siding, maroon on the first story and dark gray on the second. The resulting impression was that of an aging, genteel dame sullied by rosacea and inexpert plastic surgery.

Dad never had the money, time, or inclination to alter the low-pitched saddleback tin roof. Hail and rainstorms produced a mighty cacophony on that roof. Pigeons nestled up in the house's eaves. On summer nights, with the double-hung windows open, I was cooed to sleep by these co-residents who were joined in their chorus by the crickets, cicadas, and grasshoppers that sheltered in the tall grasses behind our house. I don't believe I have ever heard such pigeon and insect choristers again since those nights. So those moments have telescoped down to a fragment hoarded in the treasure shop of memory.

Although I never knew its specific square footage, the inner spaces of our house, if I dare call it ours, seemed generous compared to that of post World War II suburban tract houses in which we subsequently resided while I was in high school. The foot traffic flow patterns in its rooms circulated somewhat like the rabbit trails through the vegetated pasturelands on our property. Some rooms opened one onto another, requiring us to pass through one bedroom to reach a second one, or through the front room or kitchen to reach the formal dining room, for instance. The dining room had three doors opening onto the front room, kitchen, and back porch. Originally the kitchen had five entrances: from the front hallway, the dining room, a bathroom, and what we called the inside back porch as well as the door to the basement. What we called our inside back porch may have initially been a lean-to or a portion of the back porch that was walled-in before our occupation.

On our home's first level were the living and dining rooms, the kitchen, inside back porch, and one bedroom. There was also a bathroom, long but only the width of a standard-sized window, like an afterthought inserted between the bedroom and kitchen with doorways into both rooms. One of Dad's first interior improvements was to eradicate the entryway from the kitchen by building shelves for towels and toiletries into that space. Perhaps it's presumptuous to even title it a bathroom for it contained only a toilet, sink, and those shelves. Its only natural light source was its one window in the house's south wall, under which we planted tulips yearly. The space wasn't claustrophobic enough, so Dad painted it a shitty brown color. When we heard our mother use those words to describe it, David and I smiled and giggled nervously. Our feet even shuffled a skittish jig. Ladies didn't use such language and we children certainly couldn't without getting our mouths washed out with soap.

Upstairs were three additional bedrooms and a full bathroom containing a sink, toilet, and a cast iron claw-foot tub with a rolled rim. My three brothers shared one bedroom. For a time, I also slept there. The more children there were in a family, the more sharing there was going on. Even in high school, I was still encountering families in which a child slept on a bed pushed into a corner of the dining room, or the children's bedroom slept up to seven children in bunk beds. One of our upstairs bedrooms became the guest bedroom. A third room off of that was eventually transformed by my mother from a catch-all storage space into her vision of a little girl's fairy princess room. Needless to say, it was pink. I vaguely remember it also having a pink patterned wallpaper border under the cornice and gauzy white curtains with valences and tiebacks.

A staircase and banister of timeworn dark wood similar in shape to a shepherd's crook rose to the second level from slightly left of the front door. We were ordered not to, but my brothers and I found it near impossible to resist our spontaneous impulses to mount the banister at the lowest end of its curve and slide down until our little fannies bumped up against the newel post. One day I slipped while galloping down these steps and somersaulted the last few feet to land in a breathless, graceless sprawl at my father's feet. In all the nooks and crannies our house possessed, and in which my father and I might have been passing our time, fate decreed that my father's path and my own should intersect at that critical moment and in such manner.

"You deserve to fall," he told me. "That's what you get for running on the stairs." No, he didn't ask if I hurt myself or help me to my feet. He didn't even scold me. I had no wind in me to respond. I would have been too fearful anyway to try to explain away my mishap. Then he proceeded on his way. I picked myself up and did the same. No tears, no running to Mother for sympathy. I understood already that she would have none to offer me. We children were supposed to know that we should ascend and descend the stairs with the decorum of a church deacon.

Before great rooms and cathedral ceilings became architectural fads, the old Montgomery house boasted rooms with twelve-foot ceilings that were a hazard to wash, paint, or wallpaper. My parents hired a stout older woman to wallpaper the stairwell and the living and dining rooms. The sight of her on her apparatus of stepladders and planks awed my brothers and me, especially as her jerry-rigged scaffold staggered by stages up the curving stairway in the stairwell. She never made a tentative move as we monitored her progress, and we were too young to fear for her safety. The Saturday matinee at Marshall's only movie theatre couldn't have entranced us more.

When it came to choosing the wallpaper hues and patterns, either my parents' or the fifties' design preferences were skewed to field and furrow. Continuing the color motif of the shitty brown downstairs bathroom, the stairwell and front room were covered in wallpaper having a background of deep brown, which in the stairwell had a superimposed pattern of tan horizontal dashed lines. The front room featured a pattern of oversized cream-colored flowers on twisting medium brown vines. The dining room deviated from the barnyard manure theme, having instead, a repeating composition of strolling Victorian families against a moss green backdrop above the chair rail. The chair rail and the paneling below it were knotty pine.

The one north-facing window in the dining room was unique because it was our only mullioned window. It was more onerous to clean because of those multiple small panes. All the windows were difficult to clean because they stretched nearly to the ceiling while, at the same time, those on the first floor were close enough to the floor to enable us to step through them into the yard. Every one of our windows' glass panes was loose in its frame, their laxity announced by their rattling when beaten by the ceaseless prairie wind.

Our house had an attic, which was accessed through a door in the ceiling of the guest room. By hearsay it was unfinished, consisting of only the rafters. I don't remember being in it to verify that. Dad told me, "There's nothing up there for nosy little girls to see." We also had a basement, more like a partially-excavated dugout under the kitchen and downstairs bathroom. At that time, basements weren't family rooms or entertainment centers. They were furnace rooms and coal bins, rough storage lockers, and the closest refuge when tornados were spotted. Ours was all of these. I didn't enter the basement willingly because it was the domain of spiders and their webs, dimly illuminated by only one window in the south wall and a low wattage light bulb. It smelled of coal tar and must. The cleanest wall, brightened by whatever thin light the window allowed, was lined with racks holding Mason jars of Mom's home-canned fruits and tomato juice. Occasionally we huddled on the basement steps with Mom during weather suggestive of tornados. And once or twice Mom ordered me to sit down there with the creepy, crawly creatures when her frustrations with her children's energetic activities overwhelmed her customary repertoire of screaming, swearing, slapping, and spanking.

This grand old house also included Dad's sacrosanct space – his workshop. It was like a single room clad in white board attached to the back porch. Due to its compactness, it may have more closely resembled a back yard tool shed or child's play house. I think he had a large wooden workbench in there. Three of its walls accommodated one centrally situated window, and the fourth wall the door. I don't recall if Dad affixed a lock to the door. He didn't have to. He told us, his children with our clumsy and sticky, i.e. thieving fingers, that we were not allowed to enter "his" workshop – ever. I can't remember any other details of that space because all I saw of it was the door my father closed against us.

These days I avoid mentioning that the old Montgomery house, in which I spent those seven years of my childhood, was a four bedroom, two bath, ten-room house. Several listeners have surprised me by expressing the belief that living in such a sizeable house meant that my family was moneyed. But my audience wasn't with us in winter when Dad nailed plastic sheeting over the windows in an attempt to abate the wind, which encountered few barriers in its drive over the stripped corn and soybean fields. My mother would kick our mongrel, Taffy, scarred survivor of several encounters with motor vehicles, off the hot air registers in the floor. Those registers, one per room, were the only warm spot, and not very warm at that. Mom would cluster her children around her on the registers, all of us wearing sweaters or even coats. My parents were forced to install a potbellied stove in the kitchen to help ward off the chill lingering in the house's high-ceilinged rooms in winter. We had proof we were warmer inside than outside, though, because the field mice tried to move in with us during the cold months. That didn't save them. Most met a fatal end through my father's machinations. I doubt my credulous listeners had such experiences or winter guests.

Maybe today's big houses equate to big incomes or substantial inheritances. However, when the Montgomery farmhouse was built in farm country in the 1850s, large families requiring large shelters were standard. And what might have originated as small grew by additions, extensions, and add-ons. To accommodate expanding families, back porches were enclosed, lean-tos attached, separate buildings conjoined and walls thrown up or knocked down as needed. Homeowners couldn't avail themselves of architects, contractors, or tradesmen vetted by Angie's List, which didn't exist then. They built what suited their lifestyle with the materials at hand. When Dad opened some of the old walls to gain entry to the ventilation ducts, he found them wrapped in old newspapers and family letters. This was testimony to the frugality and ingenuity of previous inhabitants who utilized what lay at hand as insulation for ductwork. Additionally, these artifacts helped date the house.

And as further argument that a ten-room farmhouse isn't *ipso facto* the home of a wealthy family, I offer for comparison the home of our neighbor, the author James Jones. Jim was Marshall's richest and most famous citizen. Dad had bought the old Montgomery house in 1951 for $5,000. In 1953, after the publication of his novel *From Here to Eternity*, Jim built a house on the border of our property for $85,000. Exteriorly, Jim's home was modest in size and unpretentious in appearance even though it was the most expensive house in Marshall. Following an invitation from Jim to step inside and take a look around, Dad reported to us that, "there's only four rooms, two downstairs and two upstairs." So much for big equals rich.

4

The Land

WHEN I LIVED in Marshall, I looked upon and interacted with the land in its concrete physicality. For me the land was not a metaphor. It was not encumbered with possibilities of interpretation. The land was simply that. It was land: acres of the Illinois prairie's sable earth sprouting forbs, grass as tall as I was, and transected with drainage ditches. It anchored our house and accessory buildings; it fed our livestock; it grew our produce. Without my discerning it then, however, the land I was living on and the ecosystem I was living in was seeping into my psyche. Most people own a piece of land just as my father owned the old Montgomery house and the acreage upon which it was sited. For others of us, though, the land steals our souls, and we discover in good time that it's the land that owns us.

As an adult, Drs. Michael Jeffords and Kenneth R. Robertson's book *Illinois Wilds*,[2] the Illinois Natural History Survey website, and Ken Robertson's home page considerably fleshed out the dribs and drabs of knowledge about my natural environment that I had gleaned from my adult relatives, especially Pappy. So now I can

---

2. Michael Jeffords, Susan Post and Kenneth R. Robertson. *Illinois Wilds* (Urbana: Phoenix Publishing, 1997.

33

appreciate that prairies are a type of grassland, a landscape dominated by herbaceous plants, especially grasses. Trees are either absent
or only widely scattered on the landscape. Illinois, along with Iowa
and Missouri, is completely included in the unique biome, which
constitutes the tallgrass prairie peninsula. Bluestem, Indian grass,
switch grass and prairie dropseed comprise the matrix of the suite
of tall grasses that can attain heights of over six feet. I know that for
a fact. In spring and early summer, my brothers and I could instant-
ly disappear in our backyard meadows by simply bending over or
sitting down. This matrix of grasses also contains a wide array of
forbs, herbaceous flowering plants other than grasses, such as blaz-
ing star, mountain mint, starflowers and lupines. Prairie vegetation
becomes extremely flammable every fall, which encourages widespread fires. Prairie grasses sink deep roots, providing an anchor to
the soil and access to moisture deep underground. Natural decom-
position of these plants, particularly their root systems, and period-
ic fires added layers of organic matter to the soil, and helped create
the rich black soil of the best farming land in Illinois.

It's a far-reaching misconception that the southern Illinois
farmlands are as flat as the surface of your kitchen table. Many of
the acres given over to crops are, of course. Our own gardens, cornfields, and the holding pens by the barn for our herds and flocks
matched the stereotype. But an overview of Illinois' total land area
reveals expanses of gentle undulations as well as sporadic plunges
into gullies, some quite deep. This occurs because the area around
Marshall was never glaciated. These natural draws may contain a
pond or brook at their lowest level, and its escarpments are usually
choked with gangly young trees because their acute slopes are inac-
cessible to farm equipment.

Behind our barn on our own property was a plateau of land whose northwest edge dropped off into a ravine populated with slim saplings and years of layered leaf mold. A rill, which originated from the drainage ditch that tunneled under Second Street and formed the boundary between our side lawn and that of our great-grandfather, meandered through the several acres of our largest pig lot. From there it crossed the gravel road that connected our drive-way to our lake, cut through the lowest level of the gully where it continued nearly parallel to that same road, ingested the overflow from the lake and continued in its course to some unknown des-tination beyond the boundary of our land. The land on the other side of the brook and road flattened out somewhat into several acres of tall grass.

Our land provided the buttes and gullies, trails and lairs for my siblings and me to launch adventures spun out of our imaginations. Traversing the land's elements, we were someone else somewhere else. We were Davy Crockett and Daniel Boone; we were Indian scouts and fur traders; we were outliers.

We broke off the slender main bole of the elderberry bushes growing in what we called the big pig lot to erect the frame for teepees. But we lacked anything to substitute for buffalo skins to complete them, and our mother refused to lend us her sheets, blan-kets, or tablecloths for that purpose. When Dad heard us trying to wheedle Mom into changing her mind, he yelled at us to shut up and get out of the house. Then he accused Mom of being wrapped around our little fingers. Incentivized by necessity, my brothers and I discovered that we could slant the elderberry branches against one of the fences on our property and lay the sizeable leaves of the rhubarb plants, which sprouted in the garden every spring, across the branches to fashion a serviceable lean-to.

We played in our barn's hayloft and its pig farrowing pens blissfully oblivious, as children are, to the dustiness of the pitchforked mounds of straw and the particulate matter suspended in the shafts of sunlight falling through the warped boards of the barn's roof and walls. We roamed our hogs' enclosure and the grasslands beyond it with their apple trees; elderberry and pokeberry bushes; and weeds, grasses, and wild flowers for which we had no names. We encamped in the green cavern formed by the trunk of a large tree between the house and big pig lot that had split and collapsed in days gone by. Its branches held the fallen section off the ground as both halves of the tree continued to leaf out every spring. Grasses and weeds, including common cockleburs, further screened this cavity.

Cockleburs are herbaceous annuals whose erect stout-branched stems rise to one and a half to four feet tall. They are notable for their one-inch to one and a half inch elliptical to egg-shaped globose, or burs, with hooked spines that attach to animals' hides or people's clothing to effect their dispersal and propagation. When we discovered this curiosity about cockleburs during our first week in Marshall, David, Brad and I were charged with exuberant delight. Chicago's sedate lawns and gardens didn't have plants like this. We rotated through every coat and sweater we possessed and ran through the cockleburs until every possible garment was laden with enmeshed burs. Our maternal grandmother, our Mammoo (Helen Nauman, née Fortin wife of Harry Nauman), was visiting from Chicago to assist Mom in setting up our new home. I hope she enjoyed our hilarity as she pulled cockleburs out of yards of little coats, sweaters, and stockings, with such scant help as could be expected from her hyperkinetic grandchildren.

We tormented the crayfish, or craw daddies, as they were commonly known in Marshall which inhabited the drainage ditch. Craw daddies are fresh water crustaceans resembling small lobsters. On a visit to New Orleans as an adult, I was surprised to see that people ate them. We followed this unnamed rill in its maundering course through our fields. We waded in it where it widened and slowed its pace at the foot of the sapling-studded slope that dropped-off from the field above, and watched insects skate across its stilled surface. That was the deepest point of the stream, up to our mid calf, and well hidden from the house so that Mom couldn't see that we were doing what she had warned us not to.

When they ripened and dried, we pulled the large warty milkweed pods from their stalks and floated them like canoes down the lazy current of the stream. Milkweed, an herbaceous perennial found in fields and alongside roads, takes it name from the milky appearing juice that oozes from cut or broken stems and leaves. This white juice seals any wound to the plant because it contains latex. My brothers and I quickly learned to avoid getting it on our hands since it became sticky and elastic as it dried and couldn't be rinsed off in the tumbling waters of our runnel. The milkweed produces pods with a seam along one side that pops open when the pod ripens and dries out. Inside the pod are closely packed rolls of several hundred flat brown seeds arranged like scales on a fish, each with a folded parachute of fine silky fibers. As the parachutes open in their leisurely fashion, the wind carries away the seeds. Sometimes, boosting Mother Nature's mission, we ripped the seeds and their silk from their mother pods and blew them on their way. Since we were farm town hayseeds not interior designers, it never occurred to my mother, siblings or myself that the desiccated stems with their pods could be used in ornamental autumnal arrangements. But handily positioned as they were on the soggy banks of our nameless stream, and in our undisciplined imaginations, my brothers and I knew their destiny was to serve as sailing vessels.

Milkweeds are also the host plant for Monarch butterflies as well as a nectar source for other butterflies. I discovered that the Chicago Academy of Sciences' Peggy Notebaert Nature Museum, which opened in 1999 in Chicago's Lincoln Park neighborhood, cultivates indigenous plants, including milkweed, around its building. It does so, in part, to attract Monarch and other butterflies. We used to catch the butterflies, sometimes imprisoning them in glass jars. My elementary school teachers explained how damaging it was to capture and hold the butterflies' wings pincer style between our thumb and forefinger. I could see that, indeed, the butterflies usually were unable to fly away after we released them. Thereafter, I virtuously contented myself with admiring their vivid colors as they fluttered around me.

Another shrubby annual plant two to five feet tall reappeared in abundance every summer. Not knowing its real name, we ignorantly called these bushes pig or hogweeds because we only saw them in our big pig lot where our sows never rooted them up or ate them. David and I were, therefore, incredulous when we saw people in Chicago growing them in their yards. Since then I have learned that there are plants named pigweed, which grow as weeds or are used as fodder. There are also hogweeds, a noxious weed of the parsley family formerly used as forage for pigs. But that is not what our bushes were. Rather, as I learned later, what we had were jimson weeds or datura, a member of the nightshade family.

Jimson stems fork repeatedly into branches and, at each fork, a leaf and single erect trumpet-shaped white flower forms. They generally flower throughout the summer. The two and a half to three and a half inch long corolla, or petals, forms a whorl that has prominent ribs. The flowers only open at night, emitting a faint but pleasant fragrance, and are fed upon by nocturnal moths. After the flower withers, it is succeeded by an elliptical seed capsule one to three inches in diameter and covered with spines. At maturity, the seed capsule splits into four chambers, each with dozens of small black seeds. All parts of the plant contain dangerous levels of the tropane alkaloids atropine, hyoscyamine and scopolamine, thus, proving that our sows were wise to avoid it.

My brothers and I also trekked the road that extended through our property. It branched off Second Street to form the driveway up to and alongside our garage and terminated at the marshy edge of our lake, which was at the opposite margin of our property. It was of a multiform composition, being a distinct aggregate of white stone between the garage and house. Sparser patches of the white stones were embedded in the soil where the roadway swung left around the barn and again where it jogged right, past the lofty horse chestnut tree, and dipped down with the flank of the gully to cross the stream. From there, the road devolved to creases pressed by cars or tractors marking the path of least resistance to the lake through the acres of tall grass hillocks and around the exuberant waves of vines that, with no structural support available, engulfed patches of our untamed meadow.

This road ended its ramble at the lake. Our family always referred to it as simply "the lake." It had no other name. Years later I learned that, in the wooded gullies outside the barbed wire fence that edged our property, there were at least two other lakes. More daring than me, David had explored this area and discovered them. Since then I have also seen them, nameless like our lake, on a Google map of the area. It never entered my mind to swim in the lake. I feared being in water deeper than my ankles and to this day am shot through with a healthy fear of drowning. David and Brad were braver than me, but I don't think swimming with the water snakes in that murky liquid appealed to them either. NO SWIMMING signs were posted on the fences at the western and northern boundaries of our property where the lake was situated. Occasionally, though, Dad still caught teen-age boys from the surrounding area, including Edith's two sons, stripped naked and swimming in the lake. Dad always shouted at them to get out of the water and get off our land. My parents fretted that some foolhardy teenage trespasser might drown in our lake.

Pappy helped David, Brad and me cast fishing lines baited with worms into the lake. He and my brothers corkscrewed the fishhook through the worms' bodies while I cringed. I don't remember actually catching anything, but I doubt we were patient enough or quiet enough to while away an afternoon staring at the spot where our fishing line disappeared into the opaque water. Mammoo, Uncle Leonard and Aunt Eleanor (Mom's brother and sister-in-law) were more successful and reeled in enough trout, small mouth bass, and catfish to supply supper for a swarm of visiting relatives. Mammoo and Aunt Eleanor capably filleted the fish, dredged them in cornmeal, and fried them. They also packed filleted fish in cardboard milk cartons filled with water and froze the whole carton. Some people don't eat catfish because they're bottom feeders. But I can affirm that every one of my father's children ate everything, including fried catfish, placed on our plates. I can't say how the fish came to be in the lake. We never stocked it nor did I see any above ground streams feeding into it.

I also saw the lake serve a darker purpose. Our mongrel bitch, Taffy, was never spayed, and, like all dogs in and around Marshall, she was allowed to roam freely. We had no fenced yard in which to confine her nor did we ever walk her on a leash. In Marshall I saw more bodies of dead dogs alongside the roads than I ever saw living mutts on a leash. Predictably, Taffy produced one litter after another. My father filled a gunny-sack with one of her winter litters and heaved it out towards the middle of the lake. The lake edges were frozen but a sullen eye at its center remained ice-free. The sack landed short. No one, of course, would trust the ice shelf to bear their weight so they could walk out across its span to push the bag of puppies over its edge. I hope they froze to death quickly.

My brothers and I hunted frogs, toads, and small turtles around the lake's edge. They were likeliest to be found in the patch of common cattails near the lake's low-lying overflow. This was years before turtles stopped being merchandised in dime stores because they carried salmonella. At that time, of course, we had never heard of salmonella. We weren't very lucky at holding on to our captured amphibians and reptiles. I suspect our mother probably aided and abetted their escape.

We found the cattail plants interesting, too. They are vertical foliage with basal leaves and a simple jointless stem that bears flowering spikes. Large numbers of the tiny female flowers form a dense sausage-shaped spike up to twelve inches long and up to a little more than one inch thick. Pappy told us these spikes could be dipped in wax or fat and burned like hand-held flares. That sounded like an interesting undertaking, but Mom dissuaded us from attempting it. We tried to gather the cattail spikes like garden flowers, but the stems resisted our every effort to break them off. When ripe, the spikes disintegrate into dense cottony fluff, consisting of minute seeds less than an inch in length attached to a fine hair. Some birds use the fluff to line their nests. The seeds, like those of the milkweeds, are dispersed by the wind.

It's no longer possible to live a childhood like that. My brothers David, Brad, Gordon and I may be part of the last generation of American children for whom it was commonplace to play in a landscape in its natural state, unimproved by athletic fields, playgrounds, and manicured lawns.

⚜

Our land was sold decades ago. When I revisited Marshall in the summer of 2011, I had difficulty locating my former home and property. My husband and I walked up and down North Second Street for several minutes. Signs at the cross streets were no help to me because in Marshall in the past we delineated locations not by addresses, street names, or intersections, but by an attribute of the landscape such as just right of the county fairgrounds entrance, or by a descriptive or familial tag as, for example, the old Montgomery house. Eventually I was able to reorient myself when I recognized the drainage ditch that undercut Second Street and the swale of grass that dropped away to form the valley between what had been our side yard and that of our great-grandfather. I remembered that valley as being deeper, and, the lawn, which sloped slightly north-ward from our house and away from the walkway on the east, as being more steep than what I now saw before me. The stream was almost obliterated, reduced to an indentation in the carpet of cul-tivated grass and extending only ten feet from the egress of the red tile drain where it emerged from beneath Second Street and the sidewalk.

Onrushing time had delivered a breathtaking transformation. Everything, absolutely every other physical characteristic, was gone. The house, the barn, and the brooder house had disappeared. Of the weeping willow tree, the lilac bushes, the lilies-of-the-valley bedded under the twin Pawpaw trees no manifestation remained. Our uncultivated uncontained uncontrolled acres of land now pre-sented themselves as a respectably manicured lawn. When we made a return visit in 2013, my old home site was more updated and even less recognizable. A new Cork Medical Center and its parking lot overlay the previous site of Pop and Edith's house, the stream and a portion of what had been our side yard. The red tile drain that extended along Ash Street and plunged under North Second Street had been buried, as had our runnel into which it had emptied. Only an unostentatious slatted wrought iron dome hinted at their con-tinued presence.

Be that as it may, its altered state is irrelevant. I have committed our land and the old Montgomery house to memory where they float as close as unbidden flashbacks or as invited recall. I would like to say that every one of those buildings and living organisms of that place and time, since vanished from the tangible realm, is now fixed fast in my memory bank and is immutable. But I realize my remembrances are distorted and qualified by my lived experience since then. That which has dematerialized, but which I am attempting to recast in writing, can no longer be objective, definitive, or demonstrable with the result that the words of my story must be personal and imitative of fact.

5

The Landscape of an
Era: Togetherness

THE FIFTIES WERE all about family togetherness. People
of my parents' generation spent most of their adult life as one half
of a married couple. They married at a younger age. My mother
married at eighteen; my father was twenty. Even as late as 1962, a
number of my classmates married the day after we graduated from
the high school we attended in one of Chicago's southern suburbs.
That my mother was a full-time housewife and mother with my
father physically in absentia forty hours a week and emotionally
unavailable at all times was simply the way everybody's marriage
functioned. Pregnancy was of epidemic proportions, yet women
had as little control over their bodies as they had over anything
else;[3] "the pill" was not available until 1960. And couples stayed
married even if they were miserable. For women, divorce imposed
a heavy stigma and a financial burden. In the fifties in Marshall I
didn't know, or even know of, any divorced persons.

The general public seems to have forgotten or perhaps was never
aware that in 1955 more women were in the work force than at any

3. Karin Winegar, Introduction to *Mother* by Judy Olausen, (New York: Penguin
Studio Books, 1996).

previous time. After World War II, our government, the media, and mental health experts undertook a concerted effort to push women out of work roles they had filled in men's absence in order to ensure employment for Armed Services veterans returning from overseas. Women were not elbowed out of the work force altogether as has been commonly believed. Rather they were demoted. Thereafter, women's best chances of employment came in "women's jobs" such as secretary, teacher, nurse or librarian. The less fortunate were forced into the second tier of women's jobs as retail clerks or waitresses. In terms of both salary and respect, none of these positions paid as well as men's jobs.

Even in 1962 when I began searching for my first job, newspapers still printed sex-segregated want ads. Employers would not accept applications from women for what were deemed to be men's jobs. One company interviewer asked if I was married, which was not yet an illegal question. Then he refused to consider me for the position when I revealed that, not only was I married, but I had also wed within the previous six months. He explained his decision openly and without embarrassment, "You'd probably only stay for six months or a year, then you'll get pregnant and leave. Besides, you don't need a job. You have a husband to support you." Facing such impediments gave women an economic incentive to get and stay married.

Several years after I left home, I received an unexpected telephone call from Dad. Without preliminaries, he identified himself (This was way before caller ID.) then asked, "Are Mom and Timmy there with you?"

"No," I responded.

"Have you heard from Mom?"

"No. Are they visiting Mammoo and Pappoo?"

"I checked already. They're not there. Well, if she calls you or shows up, let me know or ask her to call me."

I agreed. He hung up. There was no polite chatter, no inquiries about my activities.

My mother later revealed to me that she had packed up Timmy and some clothes and driven to Florida. Once there, however, she couldn't find a job that would enable her to support them. Along with most of her female contemporaries, my mother paid – with the price of a curtailed education followed by a lack of marketable job skills – for her full-time early motherhood[4]. She had no education past high school and no work experience other than one year as a switchboard operator (obsolete even by the sixties), and part-time waitressing. She had no useable skills to offer an employer. She didn't even know how to type. Her only recourse in Florida was to turn around and drive back home. Thereafter, her attempt to break free was never spoken of again. If Tim ever mentioned being in Florida, she invalidated his story and his experience by telling him he must be thinking of the lake in Indiana that our family had visited.

Only after the women's liberation movement began raising our consciousness in the sixties and seventies, did we women learn that, not only had we been denied the tools and skills to earn a living, we didn't even have our own names. We were reduced to our relationships to our husbands and children. Our father's name was stuck on us when we were born, and, when he handed us off to another man at the altar, we were re-branded with our husband's name. As a young child I had so many aunts named Mary that we

---

4. Ibid.

distinguished between them by affixing their husband's given name to the Mary. So, I grew up with Aunts Mary Skeeze, Mary Lauf, Mary Ken and Mary Ted. No one, on the other hand, ever called my father Bill Elaine or my great-uncle Bill Dorothy. They were, respectively, little Bill and big Bill.

In the fifties we all sat down together every evening to eat dinner with our families. Even if we choked down what tasted like ashes and did so in smoldering silence, the point was we were eating together as a family. Our mothers made everything from scratch because that was their job. I had no idea take-out meals existed and, at least in Marshall, they didn't. Marshall had nothing even resembling fast-food joints. My parents probably would have deemed restaurant meals of any kind unaffordable anyway. That fast food might be unhealthy food had not yet surfaced as an issue.

For evening entertainment, after my mother and I washed the dishes because that was our job, we could sit in the front room and watch television together as a family. The TV screen was a picture window that helped construct the nation's self-perception. The projection of domestic life on television was a primary means of reconstituting and re-socializing the American family after World War II according to the television and film historian Mary Beth Haralovich.[5] Much of the rhetoric and imagery of postwar culture was coercive – telling Americans how to be men, how to be women, how to be parents, how to be sexual, how to be political, how to dress, what to buy, where to live, how to seem: normal.[6]

---

5. Mary Beth Haralovich, "Sitcoms and Suburbs: Positioning the 1950s Homemaker," in Private Screenings: *Television and the Female Consumer* (MN: University of Minnesota Press, 1992), 112, 114-15.
6. Anna G. Creadick, *Perfectly Average: The Pursuit of Normality in Postwar America* (Amherst & Boston: University of Massachusetts Press, 2010), 5.

There was only one TV in our home. It broadcast two channels and all shows were in black and white. Living color was not yet available. Programming ended at 10:00 p.m. After the playing of the U.S. national anthem and the television station sign-off, but while the station was still transmitting, a test pattern appeared on the screen. The test pattern was broadcast to allow television owners and repair technicians to make adjustments to the focus, resolution, and contrast of the TV's projected picture. We were not as yet afflicted with a half-dozen remotes for all the electronic gadgets we didn't yet have. If we (Dad actually) wanted to change the channel, he had to stand up, walk across the room and turn the dial on the television console. Naturally we watched the TV programs Dad wanted to watch.

It must have been in 1950 while we still lived in Indianapolis that we got our first television, which like all TVs at that time, consisted of television and phonograph components in an armoire. Ours looked like a dark wood two-door cabinet. Behind the door on the right was the twelve-inch TV screen and the knobs to turn the TV on and off, and to adjust the sound, brightness, and picture stability. That same television moved with us to Marshall. As it aged, its picture quality deteriorated. Fiddling with the knobs produced no improvements, so we adapted to viewing telecasts with lines through the picture or the continuous bottom to top scrolling of the image on the screen.

Call him Uncle Miltie or call him Mr. Television, but on Tuesday evenings we, and half the nation I guess, watched Milton Berle. His facial contortions and slapstick comedy routines, including dressing up in women's clothing, seemed hilarious at that time. I also remember watching television's earliest fare, the variety shows such as *Ted Mack's Original Amateur Hour* and *The Ed Sullivan Show*. These were superseded by half hour situation comedies like *The Honeymooners* with Jackie Gleason. I still feel antipathy toward that show. The pompous male slamming doors, shouting threats and insults – it was too much like home. I didn't have to turn on a TV to see and hear that.

Next to appear were the family situation programs, which presented a stylized view of real life. One reason so many Americans became nostalgic about the fifties was because that time was portrayed so idyllically on television.[7] We were introduced to Ozzie and Harriet Nelson and June Cleaver of *Leave It To Beaver*. June Cleaver notoriously dressed like a party hostess and always wore pearls even when doing housework. Television families were not merely a reflection of their viewers but role models for them as well.[8] They exemplified the zeitgeist of the fifties, which demanded scrupulous housekeeping and rigorous standards of dress and demeanor from women. My own mother, like all mothers that I knew personally, adhered to the defining beliefs of that time as nearly as practicable but always wore sensible cotton skirts or dresses to perform her repetitious house cleaning, cooking, and childcare routines. My mother did consider a strand of pearls a wardrobe necessity but only to be worn for an evening out.

Dad liked to view history and news programs pertaining to the Second World War. "Why does he always want to watch those?" I asked my mother. I couldn't fathom his interest in features that appeared grim or boring to me. I don't remember her explanation; I may not have understood it either. But perhaps Dad watched such fare for the same reason all the adults around me read James Jones'

---

7. David Halberstam, *The Fifties* (New York: Ballantine Books, 1994), 514.
8. Ibid, 510.

novels. Both the TV shows and Jim's books were about dramatic and significant events in which they had participated. Perhaps for many people, those were the most significant and meaningful events of their lives. And then their children's history textbooks memorialized those personal experiences. It may have imbued my parents' generation with the same amazement I experienced when I began to see the Vietnam War treated as history. For many years, it felt to me like the Vietnam War had ended just two weeks previously, and it wasn't history; it was the life I had lived.

The left side of our TV cabinet held the built in record player with a space underneath to stow my parents' ten or so twelve-inch analog vinyl plastic 33-rpm long-playing (LP) phonograph records and their few seven-inch 45-rpm records that contained only two songs. I grew up listening to Dad's country and western music. He favored Red Foley, Tennessee Ernie Ford, Guy Mitchell, and the singing cowboys: Gene Autry and Roy Rogers and Rogers' back-up singers, the Sons of the Pioneers. I don't care for county music and, now that I can make my own musical selections, I don't listen to it. For my brothers and me, it was just too bad if we didn't like Dad's preferences in television shows or music. His choice was the only choice. There was one TV and one record player. And they weren't in anybody's bedroom.

My brothers and I didn't spend the evening chatting on personal phones with our friends either. There was also only one phone that was plugged into the wall. "This isn't a toy," Dad let us know. If we had a good reason for doing so and if we asked them politely, Dad and Mom occasionally permitted my brothers and me to call Gramma and Pappy or a school friend. We shared a party line with Gramma and Pappy. I don't believe they exist any longer, but party lines were an arrangement in which two or more customers were connected to the same local line. We could determine to which household a call was being directed by a combination of short and long rings. We knew not to answer our phone on the first ring. Our signal was three short rings. Originally our phone number in Marshall was 198. Later the town's phone system was updated, after which our number changed to 5298. Gramma and Pappy had the same phone number that we did. No area codes or other prefixes were needed. Nor did I ever confront answering machines or phone trees. But, of course, I never called anyone outside a one-mile radius from our house or whom I didn't know personally.

Post 9/11 and periods of more current economic woes have prompted TV commercials and other media chatter referencing our current increased appreciation for our families. We may have lost our jobs, luxury homes, 401(k)s, and our trust and innocence, but we still have our families. In one commercial, as an example, a family enjoys each other's company during a stay-cation, camped out in a tent in their backyard.

When I was young, all our vacations were like that. Mom and Dad survived the Great Depression and the austerities necessitated by the Second World War. Their actions and reactions forever after were rooted in an unabated terror of insufficiency. Although we didn't go so far as to camp out in our yard, I'm certain our fourteen acres offered more adventure than any suburban backyard then or now. We did, though, occasionally drive to Starved Rock State Park for the day. We didn't book a room at the lodge or overnight in the cabins. Nor did we ever eat any of the refreshments offered in the park. We brought our own food with us in an ice chest and carried a blanket to spread on the ground for picnic-style eating.

Sometimes we also drove to a lake in Indiana where we waded in the shallow waves that lapped onshore, buried each other's feet in the sand, or built sand castles. I don't know which lake it was. I had heard classmates speak of the Florida coast and the ocean, so my naïve mind leaped to the assumption that we had driven to Florida. My mother laughed at me first, and then disabused me of the silly notion that we had driven to Florida and back in one day. But wherever that body of water we visited was, we did, as usual, carry our food-laden ice chest and a ground cloth with us to picnic on the beach.

On Friday or Saturday nights my parents often hosted card parties for relatives and friends. I remember Uncle Lauf and Aunt Mary Lauf being among those most frequently attending. They gathered around our dining room table, drinking beer, snacking, smoking cigarettes, and playing cards. I think they played canasta. Even David, Brad, and I had learned to play canasta so that our grandmothers would have a partner to play with during the day. But my brothers and I weren't welcome at Mom and Dad's adults-only weekend card games. We were sent to bed early to keep us out of the way. However, we were hardly able to sleep. As the night wore on, the empty beer cans filled up the trash bags, and the cigarette smoke coiled over the grownups' heads like a serpent and crept across the front room and up the stairwell. The card players' voices escalated, punctuated by eruptions of laughter. It sounded like my brothers and I were missing a rocking good time.

David and I used to tiptoe down the stairs to sit on a step near the turn of the stairway trying to peer through the balusters hoping to see or at least hear what the adults were up to. We always seemed to be found out eventually. When we heard Mom or Dad say they were going to check on the kids, we would run back up the stairs and dive into our beds feigning sleep. Dad would sternly order us back to bed if he saw us from the hallway. If he followed us up to the bedroom, though, he would tell us instead, "You little shits better stay in bed this time. If I have to come back up here, I'm going to smack you."

My brothers and I, however, spent most of our young lives in Marshall outdoors and well away from our parents' frowning eyes. Our fourteen acres of mostly uncultivated land with its animals, domesticated and feral; its fruit trees and berry bushes; its lake and overflow gully; and a brook meandering through it all were like Disney World without the entrance fee for us. To my mother, Chicago born and raised, Marshall was located somewhere between exile and Dante's *Purgatorio*. For her, our land was uncivilized nature on steroids. The animals appeared threatening. The trees and bushes dropped putrefying fruity globes that attracted pernicious yellow jacket wasps. The ever-watchful neighbors and extended family were intrusive without being helpful.

My mother and the women of her generation lived a regimented life permeated with rules and regulations not of their own devising. My mother's reputation rested on the cleanliness of her home, the sufficiency of her cooking, the demeanor and deportment of her numerous children, and the contented smile on her husband's face. Even on vacation, my mother was denied a vacation from her responsibility as the caretaker of everyone and everything.

My Aunt Eleanor had stated that she and my Uncle Leonard didn't like children. That's why they had only two children, my cousins Celeste, whose name was shortened to CeeCee, and Valerie. I was shocked. No woman in the fifties ever said that, especially out loud and to another person, even to a pre-teen such as I was at that time. To admit to holding such an opinion was so unthinkable that women probably weren't even supposed to think it. That epoch demanded familial fondness. If you didn't feel it, you needed to fake it. For women in particular, the fifties were all about suppression and pretense.

6

That Charming Idler

MY MOTHER DISMISSED her father-in-law as a charming idler who mooched off his wife's relatives. I couldn't understand then, or even now, why she characterized him that way. He was employed as a Pullman conductor on the Chicago to coastal California route, a rather interesting and out of the ordinary job in our small farming community. His schedule sent him on a cycle of ten days outbound to California, then back to Chicago followed by ten days at home. This was a conspicuous contrast to our area's farmers whose cows had to be milked every day, twice a day, and whose hogs needed their Purina hog chow and cracked corn replenished every morning. Even the town's small businesses maintained a conventional five-day 8 a.m. to 5 p.m. plus a half-day Saturday schedule. And his work gave him more to talk about than the weather and the price of hogs. My younger brothers, cousins, and I all thought my paternal grandfather was charming, too, probably in a different sense than my mother's, as well as entertaining.

When his first grandchild was born, my grandfather declared that he was too young at forty-two to be a grandfather so, henceforth, he titled himself "Pappy." Pappy attached an array of nicknames to most of his family. He called his wife, my paternal grandmother,

Clancy. His oldest son Eugene was Skeeze or Skeesicks. I have since discovered the word skeesicks in Roget's Thesaurus as a synonym for rogue. That doesn't conform to the career Army officer I remember, who demanded that his children address him as Sir and their mother as Ma'am. In Pappy's eyes maybe Skeeze was always his little boy, not as he was to me, an intimidating adult whom I didn't dare address more informally than uncle Skeeze. Pappy's second son, my father, was Polsky. Pappy's third son, Ted Leon, was always called Corny. Uncle Skeeze's two oldest children became Sue and Butch rather than being addressed by their given names of Celeste and Eugene Jr. I can't even guess the genesis of all of Pappy's designated pet names, nor why my brothers and I passed through Pappy's and our shared lives without being granted similar nicknames.

Pappy was the second child and second son of Mom and Pop's family of six sons and three daughters. He was one of only three tall people in a family of the short, the other two being my uncle Corny, and my third brother Gordon. Beset with kyphosis as he aged, he appeared to shrink ever so slightly as the increasing number of his grandchildren grew taller around him. His forehead lengthened as his hairline retreated, and his black hair ceded to gray. But his brown eyes twinkled as he observed life's amusing panorama. He was gentle, easy going and courtly. After she suffered nights of diarrhea, it was Pappy – not her own daughter – that spoon-fed his peevish mother-in-law Pepto-Bismol assuring her, "Here, mother, this will make you feel better." Bomma as she was called was a permanent, albeit not always pleasant and grateful, houseguest of Pappy and Gramma. Pappy may have affixed that familiar name to my great-grandmother. Nonetheless, he always addressed her as "Mother."

Pappy was slow moving and slow talking, as many adults from southern Illinois seemed to be. He sauntered around town acknowledging all he met with at least a smile, dip of the chin, or a drawled out, "Howdy" or "How's by you." He knew everyone and everyone knew him. Had he been a devious man, Pappy could have run for public office and coasted to victory on name recognition and good will.

Today we would describe Pappy as a raconteur. He entertained all of us with rambling tales and unexpected vignettes about our relative and neighbors, often one and the same. For instance, it was from Pappy that we learned how my father, as a young boy, shot his older brother Skeeze in the caboose (Pappy's term for it.) with his BB gun when Skeeze bent over to set up their practice target. And how Skeeze then chased Dad down the street firing his own BB gun at his fleeing little brother. Revelations like that left us wide-eyed and gape-mouthed because Uncle Skeeze and Dad's expectations for their own childrens' behavior were so stringent and inflexible.

When he was not out on the road, Pappy liked to, as he described it, putter around his house and yard while whistling to himself. He tinkered in his workshop, which was basically a workbench set up at one end of his garage. Here he made birdhouses, including a replica of his own white ranch-style home with its band of dark green around its foundation. He also assembled wind chimes from string, tape, and thin strips of glass; and weather vanes from Popsicle sticks and old aluminum muffin cups. His and Gramma's backyard was a gypsy carnival of birdhouses, wind chimes, and weather vanes. For his grandkids, Pappy concocted rudimentary paddle wheel boats from ingeniously cut plywood and a twisted rubber band. We younger Forsythes always had these little boats to sail in our bathtubs, in the drainage ditches that lined every road of our southern Illinois flatlands, and in the creek – crick as it was pronounced in Marshall – that wandered through our property. Unlike my father who forbade us to so much as set foot in his workshop, Pappy welcomed his posse of half-pint watchers and helpers.

Besides these homemade wonders from his hands and workshop, Pappy tended to give other gifts of an unexpected nature and on no special occasion, so much the opposite of the utilitarian clothing and shoes we received from our parents on Christmas and our birthdays. Pappy frequented our area's farm auctions where every tangible possession of a retiring or out-of-luck and out-of-money farm family, which could be scavenged and converted to cash, was up for bid. He once paid fifty cents for a box of miscellanea that included a covered glass dish whose handle on the lid was shaped like a donkey. We needed that like we needed another mosquito bite, but my brothers and I received it from Pappy with delight.

Another of Pappy's farm auction gifts was a goat that he transported to our house in the back seat of his car. She had disconcerting yellow eyes, forward-folding floppy ears, a little beard, and curviform horns rudely broken off before their endpoint. We unimaginatively named her Nanny. We were thrilled to have her. Mom less so, especially when our neighbors began calling to let her know, "Mrs. Forsythe, your goat is in my garden," or "Mrs. Forsythe, your goat is on my front porch." The implication being that she should do something about the reported infraction. We tried to keep Nanny corralled, and sometimes succeeded. When we weren't walking her like a well-behaved Great Dane within the confines of the big pig lot, we put a collar on her and tethered her to a utility pole near the barn.

Dad had previously unearthed a square stone pillar and grave marker somewhere on our property. He stacked them one atop the other near the barn and pigpens. Like the children around her who utilized this stack as a lookout post, Nanny also liked to stand on it. Under her cloven hooves, bunched on the tombstone, we were able to decipher in italic script not yet obliterated by time and the elements: "Far from this world of grief and sin, / With God eternally shut in." One day, though, we returned from school to discover that Nanny had vanished. While we weren't present to cry about it, Mom had sold her to the first person she could wheedle out of fifty cents.

And it was Pappy who caught a mole and brought it over to us. Perhaps Pappy also informed us how to catch them. When you glimpse a petite ridge progressing across your lawn or garden, that signals a tunneling mole. Drive a shovel blade or the tines of a pitchfork into the ground opposite the direction in which the mole is moving. You can then dig up the mole, which will have been stopped at the barricade you inserted across its tunnel. You have to act quickly and as quietly as possible. Moles speedily propel themselves backwards down the tunnel they're excavating if they detect your footsteps by means of the vibrations in the soil. Pappy confined the captured mole in a livestock water trough filled with a few inches of dirt. The mole's dark fur was a dense velvety texture. Mom warned us not to touch it. According to her, it might bite. Even if it didn't bite, it was probably lousy with germs. Like many of the animals in our lives, the mole soon disappeared. The trough remained, but my brothers and I unearthed no mole when we combed through the dirt. Since my mother was afraid to handle the "verminous rodent," she probably turned the trough on its side long enough to encourage the mole's escape. In her mind, "problem solved" – until Pappy's next interaction with her children.

We young pups, Pappy's collective cognomen for his grandchildren, benefited from his advice as well as his gifts. It was of a quite different sort than the advice we received from our mothers. My mother warned us to always wear clean underwear in case we got hit by a car, and to never take candy from a stranger who, for all we knew, might be a psychotic child abductor. Instead, Pappy whispered in our guileless ears that we could keep our treasures safe by hiding them in one of those covered receptacles in the alley. That didn't work so well in Marshall where there were almost no alleys and household detritus went into the pig stye,,the compost pile, or to the dump outside the city's boundary line. When Pappy and Gramma lived in Chicago, though, many of Dad's and his brothers' childhood trove probably vanished into the supposedly secure 55-gallon drums then utilized in the alleys.

Growing up in Marshall between the ages of seven and thirteen, I was crazy about horses and yearned to have one of my own. Numerous families in the area kept horses, even within the city limits. That being the era predating equine diapers, evidence of their presence was often seen in the streets. I was never able to convince my parents to buy me one, even though a sway-backed nag could be had for five or ten dollars. Pappy, on the other hand, assured me there was another way to make my dream come true. If I buried some of the ever-available Texas road apples, his name for horse manure, in our garden, ponies would sprout. I wished it could have been so simple, but I didn't have sufficient faith to even attempt that venture. The closest I ever came to having a horse was walking everywhere I had to go in Marshall on the next best substitute, what Pappy called my shanks' mares or shanks' ponies – my own two legs.

My brothers and I did attempt to follow Pappy's formula and directions for winemaking. We stuffed elderberries and pokeberries into Mason jars, covered them with water, screwed the lids down tight and then set them in the brooder house to ferment. I believe one jar exploded. None of us was brave enough to drink the loathsome-looking brew we produced. I never tasted the ripe berries either. My mother shrilly insisted they were poisonous. She thought that about a lot of the raw foodstuffs growing in and around Marshall, especially if it was something she had never seen on a grocery store shelf. In this case, though, she was right. Elderberries and pokeberries, if not prepared by an expert, cause gastrointestinal distress in humans. I know that birds can safely eat pokeberries; the small seeds pass through their digestive tract intact.

Whatever my mother thought of Pappy's gifts, advice, and character, he was unavoidable. Pappy, Gramma and Bomma lived in the fifth house south of us on Second Street, a newly constructed one-story ranch style house. In Marshall, it was considered modern in comparison to our own rambling, multi-room, and much-patched hundred-year-old home. When our hot water ran out or our plumbing mysteriously belched only trickles of liquid rust, Mom shepherded my brothers and me up the street in our bathrobes to bathe in Pappy and Gramma's new and more reliable bathroom.

And it would have been unthinkable to exclude them from any holiday celebration or special event. Mom did let me know, however, that she considered Gramma an ungracious hostess because

Gramma served even guests TV dinners or, if real food, it was on paper plates even at Thanksgiving and Christmas. Gramma also made us use paper cups, on the bottoms of which we had to write our initials, and we had to reuse them until they disintegrated. My mother and maternal grandmother's idea of company dinner was huge amounts of home-cooked food served on the good china with the heirloom silverware and the white tablecloth and napkins, hand-embroidered by some deceased ancestress. The preparation and cleanup required a considerable investment of time and energy. And there was always the risk that one of the children or a clumsy relative would break a piece of Great-Grandma Fortin's china or slop cranberry sauce on a tablecloth passed down through the generations. But if you didn't want to expend your best effort and risk your finest household goods –as unquestionably Gramma didn't – then you couldn't hold yourself forth as a hostess.

One enigma David and I could never unravel was how the charming, gentle, and humorous Pappy came to be married to the ill-tempered and hypercritical Gramma. Nor could we understand how Pappy could have produced the harsh, selfish, and mean-spirited man our father was. Instead, Dad inherited Gramma's love of teasing, abusive teasing against which children are too unsophisticated and inarticulate to defend themselves. When Dad and Gramma were together, they seemed to reinforce each other viciousness in subjecting us children to a withering barrage of ridicule. Time is merciful and has blotted out their exact words, although I vaguely recall that those pertaining to me were that I was fat and had a bad complexion and that Brad was a bed-wetter. What I do remember is my cringing in humiliation. I could only stare at the floor through tear-filled eyes incapable of responding, hoping for rescue by someone else of the supposedly nurturing adults to whom fate had abandoned me.

I measured the events in my life by where I lived and how many brothers I had when they occurred. When Pappy died in February of 1968 at the age of sixty-eight, I was twenty-four years old, living in Chicago, and my fourth and youngest brother Timothy was ten. I made the three-hour drive from Chicago to Marshall for Pappy's funeral with my cousin Sue. During our journey she convinced me to enter Pappy and Gramma's house in front of her in order to deflect the wrath of her parents, my Uncle Skeeze and Aunt Mary. Like many young people in the sixties, Sue had became discontent with her easeful suburban family routine and sought to reinvent herself by abandoning her husband and two young daughters. She moved to Chicago to take up a job and undertake a life that was more meaningful than keeping house and caring for her husband and children. Like many parents in the sixties, Uncle Skeeze and Aunt Mary were unhappy with their oldest daughter's incomprehensible choices. It may have been the Age of Aquarius, but flouting convention still wasn't for anyone concerned about the opinions of others. Even at the age of twenty-six, Sue still addressed her parents as Sir and Ma'am and cowered when they glared at her in frustrated fury.

That conversation in the car with my cousin and the dark looks Aunt Mary cast upon her miscreant daughter when Sue and I breached the knot of gathered relatives in Gramma's front room are among the fragments that I remember of Pappy's funeral service. In fact, there were two services, the first being a Masonic ritual. Most of my adult male relatives were Masons and Uncle Skeeze was a Shriner. During their ritual, the Masons closed and moved

Pappy's coffin. I felt uneasy about that, thinking how Pappy was being smothered and jostled. At the evening's conclusion I remember my mother and aunts taking hold of Gramma's arms and pulling her away as she looked, longingly I thought, across the room at the casket. I sensed that she wanted one more last close look, and to lay her warm hand over Pappy's still fingers before their separation in this world.

During Pappy's second funeral service the following day, Timmy started crying. Without speaking, I moved over, put my arms around him and hugged him. Our mother turned to him, too, and hissed, "Shut up. Seeing you cry will upset Gramma." Afterwards, Mom dismissed Timmy's emotional display as a result of fatigue. "After all," she explained to me, "Timmy never lived in Marshall and barely knew Pappy, so he couldn't be distraught about him dying."

I can't remember crying or feeling sad or feeling much of anything when Pappy died. Regardless of my lapse of memory, Pappy's death warranted tears and lamentation at his loss while rejoicing in the memory of having been related to a worthy man. Every young person should have a Pappy. He was a child magnet. He had no agenda, no prerequisites for his flock of grandchildren except to enjoy our shared lives. At a time and place that often felt to my young self like a mission behind enemy lines, he was fun and funny and simply charming. He gained what we probably all yearn for: his life was not an irrelevant whisper into the immeasurable void; his life mattered to us, his death grieved us, and we remember him with love and laughter.

7

Three or Four Things Every Little Girl Must Have

THE SINGLE ADVANTAGE I gained as the only daughter in a bunch of brothers that eventually increased to four was having a bedroom of my own in Marshall. Given its special status as unshared sleeping quarters and how the idea of a little girl's pink bedroom was so dear to my mother, it's interesting that I now find myself barely able to remember the features and contents of my room. I know it was large with two windows, one with a view over the roof of the inside back porch and onto the pig lots. The other window, facing north, overlooked the brooder house and the roof of Dad's workshop.

My pink bedroom contained my Hollywood bed and a wooden chest of drawers. Most likely my two or three dolls in their doll bed also resided there, present but ignored. Why would I be interested in dolls when I was followed into life and everywhere thereafter by my crowd of attention-demanding, diaper-filling, and crying younger brothers? Mammoo and my mother sometimes admitted that they realized as much. But dolls and their paraphernalia were simple-minded gift solutions for little girls, and I'm sure my mother found it hard to resist that era's prescription: little girls couldn't have imagination-enhancing playthings like Lincoln Logs and Tinker Toys; girls must have dolls.

One particular thing that I remember best about the pink bedroom was the occasion one spring or summer day when Mom and I drove out on some errand. She had just painted that room and left the windows open wide to ventilate the paint fumes. While we were away from home, an unexpected squall blew through town. My mother rushed home fretting, "I hope it's not raining into my just-painted room." With windows on the second floor of the northwest corner of the house left agape, that was a vain hope. And, after one hundred years, the bedroom floor sagged into its least supported point. Not only had rain blown in, but it had also collected in a noticeable pool in the middle of the room. I don't remember everything my mother had to say when confronted with that, but she did tell me, as she sometimes did, "Don't mention this to your father." The pool of rainwater was sufficient to justify buckets, so we scooped up the water and threw it out the west window onto the flat roof of the inside back porch below. Fortunately, the wood floor was covered with a sheet of linoleum, which functioned like a pool liner. Rags wrung out the window soaked up the final film of wetness and any proof that Mom had been so foolish as to leave the house with the windows yawning open to the elements. Any farmer could have appraised the color of the sky, the mass and movement of the clouds, the texture of the ambient air, and the manner in which the wind shifted the tree leaves and predicted an approaching rainstorm. After living in Marshall for seven years, I could, too. Regardless, that little misadventure went unheralded.

In addition to the pink bedroom, my mother also believed little girls should have curly hair. My hair could be described then and now as very slightly wavy, and that's on a day with a high level of water vapor in the atmosphere. But my poor mother tried. She pestered her older brother Leonard, a licensed beautician, and his wife Eleanor into styling our hair with boxed home permanents. At various times, he and Aunt Eleanor owned and operated beauty salons, at least one of which was located in Chicago's Beverly neighborhood. When we were growing up, David and I never knew what color Aunt Eleanor's hair really was. It varied from brunette to ruddy to platinum. When our families lived in close proximity, Uncle Leonard and Aunt Eleanor would periodically commandeer the kitchen and/or bathroom and assail our nostrils with their potions and scrape Mom's scalp and mine with their implements so that my silhouette was transformed from silky Afghan hound to permed poodle. My mother emerged beautified fifties style with auburn-tinted forward-flounced curls and a slightly left of center roll of bangs. Our refreshed look made Mom happy. I'm not sure that my aunt and uncle were paid for their off-the-clock work, but all the adults had a jovial afternoon drinking beer, smoking cigarettes, and swapping stories.

For a time, Mom fell into the habit of sending me weekly to get my hair styled by a hairdresser, who operated her business out of her home. And this was when she was sending David and Brad to the barbershop on a weekday after school to get their 1950s crew cuts. She admonished them not to lose the two quarters she doled out to each of them. It saved her not only time but money to trust them to reach the barber on a Monday through Thursday afternoon with the fifty-cent price of a haircut still in hand rather than to take them there herself on Saturday when the cost of a boy's haircut rose to $1.25.

I also overheard Mom on the phone negotiating with the hairdresser to have her own hair cut and styled. "Will you take a dollar off if I wash my hair myself at home? And how about fifty cents if I bring my own hair rollers?"

I winced in embarrassment to hear her dickering in this way to get nickels and dimes knocked off portions of the stylist's services. She could have used the money squandered on my hair curling sessions to get her own hair cut and styled. Since I was painfully self-conscious, I was happier slipping quietly through life unnoticed. I wouldn't have minded if my untended hair always hung nearly to my eyelashes and hid half my face as it does in my second grade elementary school photos. I was equally satisfied with wearing my hair pulled back in that ubiquitous fifties hairstyle – an uncomplicated ponytail sprouting from the crown of my head.

At that time, I was still oblivious to the post World War II presumptions that women now had the prosperity and the leisure with which to primp. Following the restraints of the Great Depression and a world war that enlisted every United States citizen in its execution, women during the fifties could return to being women who cared about presenting a pleasing appearance to their men. And, obviously, that visual impression mattered to my mother. But I began to deduce that, for my family, prosperity and leisure were elusive assumptions. Our home permanents, weekday crew cuts and bargaining with beauticians, among other details of our family life, were pinpricks of perception on my part that apples, pears, and such grew on our trees but not money.

Ballet lessons were another must-have for little girls according to my mother. Piano lessons were desirable, too. As in most small communities, there were one or two women who taught rudimentary gymnastics and dance and others who gave music lessons. In Marshall, these dance instructors were Miss Nancy Sauer and Martha, whatever her last name was. I cannot remember my piano teacher's name at all. That's probably indicative of my skill and interest in these pursuits.

My anonymous music teacher offered piano lessons at her own house, which was on Marshall's south side. Her students were not allowed to enter any further into her home than the front parlor, where she kept the piano for our instruction. Incredibly, an upright player piano, which my mother nagged me to practice on, appeared in our front room almost simultaneously with the piano lessons. I have no recollection of how we acquired ours. Pappy may have bought it for us at one of the farm auctions he frequented. I can't believe Dad would have bought us a new piano.

Player pianos, such as ours was, contain manually-controlled, pneumatically-operated piano-playing mechanisms. A large lever beneath the keyboard switched the one we possessed from manual to automatic. My brothers and I were more interested in trying to insert the roll of perforated paper into the apparatus which enabled the piano, or pianola as it was also called, to play automatically than we were in learning how to play the instrument ourselves. These pianola rolls consist of continuous sheets of paper rolled onto a spool, which fits into the player piano's spool box. The free end of the music sheet hooks onto a take-up spool, which unwinds the roll across the tracker bar (the reading mechanism). Perforations on the paper programmed the musical score. My piano lessons were short-lived, maybe because I was so clearly lacking in musical ability. I don't recall the fate of our piano, which, in our home, was more of a dust attractant than musical instrument. By the 1950s, the manufacture of pianolas had dropped precipitously. Without a doubt, I didn't help keep them in business.

The ballet classes were more interesting. Martha also taught in-house on the enclosed front porch of her parent's home. I studied with Martha after Miss Sauer closed her dance studio and because my friends did. Miss Sauer had a dance studio with a ballet barre and mirrors in a commercial building uptown on Archer Street. There, I learned a primitive gymnastics of somersaults and cartwheels appropriate for grade school age pupils. I also studied tap dancing and ballet. That my companion bun heads and I and the dance studio itself were not professional was demonstrated by the fact that we galloped from soft leather ballet slippers to box-toed pointe shoes in less than two years. We yearned to advance to the more impressive toe shoes without enduring the requisite groundwork for performing Swan Lake balanced on our toe tips on a block of wood. Miss Sauer allowed this. I don't know if her understanding was as deficient as that of us and our parents, but she doubtlessly did know that bored farmers' daughters and their money don't keep coming back to perfect perfunctory *port de bras* and *ronds de jambe* at the barre in ballet slippers.

In addition to our mundane weekly classes, we students participated in music and dance recitals staged by our teachers. These served several purposes. They allowed our teachers to showcase both their pupil's budding talents as well as their own more mature artistry. Plus, such events pleased our parents and demonstrated what their lesson fees were buying. These recitals were held, not at our respective teaching sites, but at various Marshall churches and the lodges of the town's fraternal and fellowship orders.

I can recall taking part in only one piano recital, which presented my mother with an opportunity to dress me up and curl my hair. I played a little ditty, something on the order of "Twinkle, Twinkle, Little Star." Looking back on that musical juvenility, I should be blushing to remember even that much. I found the dance recitals more engaging. I remember primping and donning our costumes in Miss Sauer's studio. Its storefront windows and the clear glass pane in the door were papered over for privacy's sake. We student performers were ordered to strip down to our underwear and were smeared with thick liquid makeup after which we were helped into our ensembles. I was so self-conscious at that age – approximately eight to eleven – that I wished I had been diverted into the cloakroom or changing room in which the more physically-developed young ladies were allowed to prepare. I can't recall how we moved between the dance studio and the performance venue. We may well have traveled on shank's mares, or our own two legs, since wherever we were going to perform was within the approximately four square blocks of Marshall's uptown.

In class, we wore the traditional black leotard and pink tights. For most dance performances, I was attired in a classical pink tutu with its fitted bodice and skirt of short stiff layers of netting projecting horizontally from the waist. For one of my dance recital numbers, I was afforded the privilege of wearing a pseudo-gypsy dress and headband, hand-sewn by my mother from a McCall's, Simplicity, or Butterick pattern. We saved my gypsy outfit, and in succeeding months I wore it for Halloween parties and trick-or-treating.

With her hand-held point and click Kodak Brownie camera, my mother memorialized my first try-on of my pink tutu and pink pointe shoes. As the westering sun slashed through the front windows of our house, she captured me posed on tiptoes, my lips reddened with borrowed lipstick, and my long, dark ponytail pulled forward over my left shoulder. Behind her, my father snickered, "She looks like a pink sow in a pink tutu."

My family raised swine for Chicago's slaughterhouses. We had at least three Chester White sows with their piglets in our barn and pig lots when that moment was preserved in my mother's photograph and my memory. Sows, even our own, weren't Miss Piggy nor were they the three little pigs of folktales. They were as big as an old-fashioned wood office desk, low-slung and solid, weighing in at three hundred pounds at the least. I had, by that age, entered my preadolescent chubby stage, but if Dad was referencing body mass index, I don't think anyone even then would have considered me overweight.

The many years since then have erased any other memories of that moment, so I don't know how my mother and I responded to his remark. Mom may have cried out, "Bill!" in protest, but at the very same time maybe the corners of her mouth turned up baring her front teeth in an unsuppressed smile. Perhaps, once he brought it to her attention, my mother also saw how clearly I did resemble one of their bulky Chester White sows reared up on its hind legs but with a pink tutu instead of the usual belt of white skin circling its antique rose colored midriff. Perhaps, at that moment, she no longer looked at me with a mother's eyes but with the eyes of a woman posing as a man's appreciative audience. I was twice wounded if I witnessed Mom smile, corroborating her husband's assessment.

My mother died before I could ask her if, when she was growing up, she had all of the things she attempted to press upon me – the pink bedroom, the professionally-styled ringlets, and the piano and ballet lessons. Thus, I never discovered whether that was what made her believe such things were likewise imperative for her own daughter. Or, maybe, she didn't have any of them. So that made her want to ensure that I did receive them as recompense to the deprived little girl she had been, and to make available to herself the possibility of experiencing vicariously that which she had previously been denied.

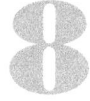

8

My French Connection

MY MATERNAL GRANDMOTHER was my own personal French connection. My brothers and I grew up knowing our mother's parents as Mammoo and Pappoo. Mammoo was short and round with wavy dark hair. She gazed upon us with the brown eyes of a devoted beagle. Pappoo was tall and bony with slicked-back gray hair. His glacial blue or gray eyes peered at the daily financial columns of his newspaper through frameless glasses. Although I can't say from where we derived their pet names, they may be approximations from the French language and mean something like Mama and Papa. Mammoo's family were French Canadians who lived in Beaverville, Illinois, which is about ninety miles south of Chicago and eight miles west of the Illinois–Indiana state line.

According to the village legends of Beaverville's founding, thirty-two families from the Canadian province of Quebec sailed down the St. Lawrence River and across the Great Lakes. They stopped at Fort Dearborn, now Chicago, and then pushed southward through the swamp and prairie until they reached an area of good land and numerous creeks where they established a settlement in the spring of 1853, which they named Ste. Marie. This group was comprised mostly of newly-married or single members of the Fortin, Dionne, and Boudreau families as well as at least six Arseneau families. The village was originally platted on land owned by Charles Arseneau. In 1905, when they realized another town in Illinois had the name St. Mary, the village founders changed the name of their town to Beaverville. That name was inspired by the profusion of beavers in the area in the early 19th century at a time when Beaver Lake across the border in Indiana still existed.

Beaverville is the home of St. Mary's Catholic Church, and to this day its only church. Prior to 1857, services were held in the homes of parishioners. A priest came from L'Erable to offer the Holy Sacrement when St. Mary's was first built in 1857. Ste. Marie was a mission of L'Erable, Illinois, which is just west of Beaverville and was also founded by French Canadians in 1853 and 1854. L'Erable was platted but was never incorporated. The Rev. Epiphanie Lapointe came from Canada in 1857 as Ste. Marie's first resident priest. By 1858 roughly fifty families were worshiping in the church built on twenty acres of land donated by Charles Arseneau. In 1859 a rectory and the entrance to the church were built, and the church was enclosed with a fence. All records of baptisms, marriages and burials were kept in L'Erable prior to 1859. The first baptism recorded at St. Mary's Church was that of Amos, son of Marcel Fortin and Philomine Fortin, née Francoeur on November 16, 1859. Amos was Mammoo's father.

Mammoo, her four brothers and four sisters attended Holy Family Academy, which was directed and staffed by the Sister Servants of the Holy Heart of Mary. Mammoo reminisced how the nuns would follow them around at recess to prevent the siblings from speaking to each other in French and would rap their knuckles with a ruler if they did. At home, her family only spoke French.

Mammoo claimed that she didn't learn English until she entered Holy Family Academy's first grade. Like those nuns, Pappoo never allowed any foreign language – and he considered that any language other than English – to be spoken in his home. That may explain why my mother was not adept in learning foreign languages. However, the Fortins, including my mother, continued to speak French amongst themselves while Grandma Fortin was alive. A French word or phrase spoken by one of them was like skipping a stone across a pond, creating widening ripples of French until their whole conversation had veered from intermittent French words to exclusively French. The Holy Family grade school closed in June 1965. The high school was active until June 1969 when it too closed. The buildings were razed in 1975 and 1976.

August 29, 1909, the Rt. Rev. A. J. McGavick laid the cornerstone for the present St. Mary's Church. Its architect was Chicagoan Joseph Molitar. The church's 1911 dedication book described the church's interior as Corinthian in design. According to the dedication book, the church has a seating capacity of 1,200 and its dome is fifty-three feet in diameter. My husband and I visited St. Mary's Church and Cemetery in July 2013. The church seems huge, larger than needed for both its original communicants and now for a parish of fewer than one hundred participating families.

The exterior of the church, which the 1911 dedication book charitably characterized as Ionic, is built of Bedford stone with a roof of French red clay tile. As past members of the Chicago Architecture Foundation, my husband and I notice the characteristics of built structures. So to be more precise, St. Mary's exterior is a gallimaufry drawn from Romanesque, Renaissance, and Byzantine styles. Its massiveness and red roof make St. Mary's visible for several miles. It is affectionately known variously as the "Cathedral in the Cornfields," the "Cathedral in the Country," and the "Prairie Cathedral."

St. Mary's stained glass windows were one of the contributing factors for the church being placed on the National Register of Historic Places on May 6, 1996. The stained glass windows, which not surprisingly depict the life of the Blessed Virgin Mary, are not signed. No record has been uncovered which identifies their designer or originating studio. An uncommon feature of the windows is their extensive use of opalescent glass. They have been protectively glazed since their installation in 1911. Since 1991, St. Mary's Church Preservation Society has invested $1,380,000 in restoration of the church. Of that sum, $320,000 was the cost for restoring the stained glass windows, an undertaking that began in June of 2001 and was completed in the summer of 2004. The time and dollar amounts invested bespeak an impressive level of commitment from the parish and Holy Family Academy alumni.

David, Brad and I visited Great-Grandma and Grandpa (Philomene and Amos) Fortin in Beaverville with our mother. Every bedroom in their two-story wood frame house contained brass beds, every one of which seemed to feature a noticeable well in the middle of its mattress. At night, bedmates found themselves rolled into an entwined embrace in this mid-mattress pit. I was quite impressed to observe how grandma Fortin cooked all the family's meals on a cast-iron stove. And she had done so while raising eleven children, nine of whom survived to at least the age of twenty-one. Their backyard was almost wholly given over to their garden. They grew tomatoes as we did but theirs were yellow instead of red. My Fortin relatives assured me that yellow tomatoes were sweeter than the red varieties. Not taking anything for granted, Grandpa Fortin also sprinkled sugar on his sliced tomatoes. He said the sugar offset the tomatoes' acidity. In my opinion, nothing improved the taste of any color tomato, which, at that age, I didn't like.

My mother also brought five-year old David, four-year old Brad, and me with her when she drove to Beaverville in October of 1951 for the funeral of Grandma Fortin who died at age eighty-four. Grandma Fortin's body was laid out in an open coffin in the front sitting room of the house she and Grandpa Fortin had shared in life. The nuns from St. Mary's Church and Holy Family Academy attired in their drab black habits cinched at the waist with rosaries, and their bowed heads curtained in equally dreary black wimples, knelt on the adjoining front room floor praying in Latin or French. I wouldn't have understood either. Their hands cradled prayer books, or their fingers plied strands of rosary beads. Like the ignorant, un-churched seven-year old that I was then, I tiptoed through their kneeling, muttering, sooty cluster when I wanted to enter or exit through the front door.

During an unsupervised interval, I gathered with three or four other young girls also present for the funeral to entertain ourselves in front of Grandma Fortin where she lay displayed in her casket. The furniture had been removed from the room except for the table upon which Grandma Fortin's casket rested, so we sat on the floor to play a version of pass the button. One girl sat or stood with her back to the row in which the rest of us had arranged ourselves. When she turned around and cried out, "Button, button, who's got the button?" she had to guess who was holding the button. We didn't have a button handy so we substituted a rosary, of which there was no lack. When I was the girl caught holding the rosary, I pulled what I thought was a clever trick. I stuffed the rosary under my buttocks, and then held out my empty hands like the others. Some moments of laughter and confusion ensued – that is until I confessed. The other girls were horrified. They behaved as if I had exposed my bald pudenda to beloved mother. Their reaction was understandable. On that particular day, I was probably the only female in Beaverville who had not been educated by Catholic nuns. I don't recall what punishment was meted out for my transgression. My mother, I'm sure, was too distracted by the loss of her grandmother to tackle the matter of a rude girl sitting on a rosary.

A priest tolling a hand-held bell, and the company of nuns and mourners escorted Grandma Fortin's closed casket from the house. The priest led her final retinue up the sidewalk, then across the street and into St. Mary's Church for the funeral mass. My mother attended the funeral service and accompanied her grandmother's body to its gravesite in St. Mary's Cemetery behind the church. My brothers and I remained under supervision at our great-grandparents' house. Interestingly, I can't remember my own grandmother Mammoo being present. Her actual absence from her own mother's funeral liturgy would have been hard to fathom. It is conceivable, however, that the ever-churlish Pappoo ordered her to stay home in Chicago to take care of him.

When my mother returned from the church and cemetery, she sat down on the back steps of Grandpa Fortin's house and started crying. My brothers and I were alarmed. We didn't know what to say or do. Adults didn't cry. I had even asked Mom why she and adults in general never cried, even about things that I thought were sad. "It's because we've experienced so many disappointments, losses, and misfortunes by the time we reach adulthood that we've run out of tears," was her explanation.

⚜

When people reminisce about the families that supposedly existed in the good old days, Mammoo is the grandmother they're envisioning. She would have rather snipped off her tongue with her pinking shears than ever disagree with anyone. She was cheerful and infinitely patient. She deemed all of her seven grandchildren to be remarkable. Our trivial chatter was fascinating, our most senseless activities delightful, our pouting and sulking charming. She made us feel like there was nothing she would rather be doing than baking cookies with us, window-shopping on Michigan Avenue with us, running through the lawn sprinkler with us. As we matured, she became a pen pal to the letter writers, a conversationalist with the talkative, a library patron with the readers, and a card shark competing against those of us who learned to play canasta.

She was an excellent cook while her daughter, my mother, could hardly boil water without scorching it. Mammoo could have a pan of thin-cut bone-in pork chops frying on her stove's back burner for half a day, and they still emerged tender and toothsome. If my mother had cooked them, those same pork chops would have had the taste and texture of rawhide dog chews. Preparing a holiday feast for a dozen or more family members didn't intimidate Mammoo. Little could be more glorious in her estimation than a roomful of exuberant diners and drinkers. She herself often did not sit down with her guests until coffee was poured after dinner. "I tasted so much of what I was cooking that I'm not even hungry anymore," she would tell us. Instead, she would pace back and forth behind our chairs urging us on with cries of, "Eat! Eat! Bill, have more turkey. Eleanor, finish that little bit of cranberry sauce, so I can refill the bowl." If anybody left Mammoo's table hungry, they must have arrived with their jaws wired shut.

With almost saintly good will she also catered to Pappoo's finicky appetite, preparing three meals a day, three hundred and sixty-five days a year for him because he didn't ingest any edibles he could fix himself. He was as fussy as a teething baby. Since she was never certain what side dishes might tempt him on any given evening, she served his meat on a dinner plate and arranged up to six small plates and bowls around that with a few tablespoons of varying vegetables and canned fruits in each one. Mammoo received no appreciation for her efforts. "Please" and "thank you" were words not to be found in Pappoo's vocabulary. He ate whatever he ate with his face buried in the stock market reports that he ripped from the newspaper and tucked under his eating utensils. My grandparents hadn't read about the Great Depression in a history book; they lived it. So if Pappoo left so much as one tablespoon uneaten, Mammoo lovingly wrapped it in wax paper and stowed it in the refrigerator until it could be brought forth for his next meal. My parents were the same way and for the same reason.

After she and Pappoo retired to a cottage in the woods near Rhinelander, Wisconsin, and I was employed in Chicago, Mammoo made me dresses, skirts, and blouses appropriate for the nice office jobs I held and where I worked with hands that stayed clean, and also colorful beaded and sequined festive party wear. Usually, I was unaware she was creating anything for me until it arrived in my mailbox. Every outfit always fit perfectly. I don't know how she did it. I wasn't present for her to measure me. She often made clothing for me from remnants of fabric left over from her other projects. When visiting her, I was likely to chance upon the chair uphol-stered with the same material from which she made one of my skirts. She assembled a patchwork lap throw for me that contained cloth scraps from the decorative pillow covers I saw on her sofa and from a bathrobe she had sewn for herself. Mammoo produced all of these on her antique treadle Singer sewing machine or by hand stitching them. The nuns at Holy Family Academy had taught her to sew stitches so small and even they were harder to pick out than seams sewn by machine.

Mammoo was artistic, too. The sole wall decorations in Mammoo and Pappoo's apartment in Chicago and their cabin in Wisconsin were about a dozen of her charcoal sketches. She signed them with her maiden name, Helen Fortin, and they are profession-ally framed. My brothers and I divided them amongst ourselves when we came into possession of them after both Mammoo and our mother passed away. I was able to obtain my two favorites. One is a still life of a bowl of fruits on a table draped with a ruched ivory cloth. The other features a barely discernable two-wheel track past two mature trees and shorter darker foliage massed behind them. Over the years, my youngest brother Tim has grabbed Mammoo's drawings that David and Gordon originally chose. Tim periodical-ly accused me of not properly caring for and displaying Mammoo's artwork, and even threatened to drive into Chicago and physi-cally wrest them away from me. I haven't talked to him for several years. He's an alcoholic and a drug user with whom, in my opinion, it's impossible to carry on a coherent conversation. But, since he seems to value the idea of possessing our grandmother's art, I have designated my two framed charcoal sketches to him in my will. So if he survives me, he can have my Mammoo's artwork over my dead body, so to speak.

When Mammoo passed away, Pappoo turned on his spigot of crocodile tears and ramped up the dramatics, "Oh, my dear Helen, my beautiful Helen. What will I do without her?" he wailed.

Two of Mammoo's surviving sisters, my great aunts Esma and Zella, glared him into silence. No one had to be a clairvoyant to see that Pappoo, for as long as anyone could remember, treated his dear beautiful Helen with the indifference one would accord to a servant automaton. Everything in their lives had to be done his way on his timetable. Mammoo couldn't undertake any activity or family visit that disrupted her cooking or cleaning for him. He refused to take her to the doctor when she was ill, even when she developed pneumonia. When they lived out in the Wisconsin woods, he forbade her to walk up the road to drop in on the few neighbors who lived there year round as they did. Then he forbade her to row their rowboat along the shore to visit the lodge and hunters' cabins around the bend of the lake. It was only when my mother or her grandchildren vacationed with her that Mammoo was able to socialize with neighbors or the owners and guests of the lodge. She was forced to hide her cigarettes in the trees of the encircling woods when Pappoo decided he would quit smoking. Actually, he quit buying cigarettes for himself and smoked Mammoo's instead – except for those she was able to conceal.

Pappoo would do just fine without his dear beautiful Helen. Any servile female could serve him equally well. Eliciting no sympathy from his hostile sisters-in-law, they of the steely spines and chilly frowns, Pappoo looked to my mother, the daughter who still craved fatherly affection from him. He begged my mother to take him in. He claimed he could sleep on the living room sofa, and he wouldn't eat much.

Pappoo and my father were almost equally self-centered and oblivious to anyone else's needs, but Pappoo was also extremely, unselfconsciously fidgety. Sitting at the supper table, Pappoo would pick up a piece of silverware and start tapping it against his glass while simultaneously shifting his body about on his chair, crossing and uncrossing his legs. He didn't do this to attract attention. He seemed unaware that he was doing it at all. But he was an adult and other adults were always present, which prevented Dad from smacking him or yelling at him to shut up. Instead, Dad would pick up Pappoo's silverware and hold onto it until Pappoo had food on his plate that required utensils. It didn't help to remove Pappoo's glass. He would tap his knife, fork, or spoon against his plate, and squirm like a little boy who needed a potty chair.

Dad refused to allow Pappoo to spend so much as one night in his house. My poor mother was trapped between the two most abusive males she ever knew. My relationship with my mother was increasingly contentious as I entered adolescence, but on this issue my sympathetic response was pure instinct. When she repeated to me her father's entreaties and her husband's dictates, the first words I blurted out were, "Pappoo's trying to make you feel sorry for him. Mommy, don't let him do that." What I didn't say to her was that, as far as I was concerned, her father didn't merit disquiet from her. Be that as it may, her husband's evil temperament carried more weight than her father's lamentations. Mom moved Pappoo into a retirement home.

⬥⬥⬥

Grandma Fortin's passing saddened my mother, but Mammoo's death destroyed her. I can totally understand this. Mammoo died in November of 1979. My mother died unexpectedly on May 1, 1980 at the age of fifty-five. My mother's death was a wound so grievous as to fall beyond the bounds of rational response. I felt as if the wheels had come off the chariot, as if the fire on the hearth had been dashed out, as if the universe had spun loose of its tether. I had a migraine for two weeks. I didn't think I could ever stop crying.

I believe that my mother often compared herself unfavorably to her own mother simply because Mammoo seemed content within the prescribed parameters of her life. My mother, however, experienced the same manner of life as confining and unsatisfying. And no matter how much my mother drank, her life didn't look any more meaningful. The contempt and rebukes lobbed at her by my father and brothers didn't inspire her to try a different path. My heart hurts when I remember how she was suffocated by the life she felt compelled to live. My mother wanted to be her mother, but I never wanted to be my mother.

9

God Is Like Your Father

"GOD IS LIKE your father," a Jesuit priest at Loyola University informed me.

"God forbid," was my response.

───✦───

Some elements of that incident, let me call it the sandwich incident, are eidetic. I can conjure them up with substantial clarity. Other details have melted into shadowy realms beyond my recall.

I was in the kitchen of our house in Marshall with my brothers David and Brad. My mother was absent. I was eight years old then, so I'm guessing she must have been in the Terre Haute, Indiana hospital after giving birth to my third brother Gordon. Almost the only occasions my mother wasn't home with her children were when she was in the hospital birthing more of them. And that's also why I, rather than our mother, was making lunch for my brothers and myself.

I remember that kitchen well. Its ceiling at that time might still have been half white and half red. My parents had to replace the electrical wiring throughout our hundred-year-old house. Holes had been punched in the kitchen ceiling to access some of the electrical conduits and junction boxes. My parents painted the patched and completed portion of the previously white kitchen ceiling red, an unusual choice for the fifties. I can't even offer a conjecture as to who made that decorating decision. Lacking time or money for its completion, the unfinished portion of the ceiling remained so, fenestrated and oyster shell white, for an extended period of time.

The kitchen was large enough to be called an eat-in kitchen, a description I never heard at the time. It still had three of its four original doorways. Only the entryway onto what we called the inside back porch was fitted with a door, kept closed during cold weather. A wide doorway as well as a cut out pass-through pierced the wall separating the kitchen from the dining room. That wall and the lower portion of both rooms were paneled in knotty pine. For years afterwards, I regarded knotty pine as the stigma of the fifties and the lower working class.

I was standing at our well-worn kitchen table assembling peanut butter and jelly sandwiches on a wood cutting board scored with years of service. I laid out six slices of Wonder bread. I had no idea any other kind of bread existed, unless you baked your own as my paternal great-grandmother occasionally did. Mom rotated her selection of jams and jellies. That day's available flavor was cherry jam. As to peanut butter options, we had not progressed beyond the original creamy.

I applied margarine mindlessly – I can't fathom now why we needed an underlying layer of that too – and then peanut butter and jam to four of the slices of bread, after which I pressed them together to complete my brothers' sandwiches. I cut their sandwiches in two diagonally and served them on plates to David and Brad who were seated to either side of me at the table. This was the procedure, the form and components of which could not be deviated from: apply margarine from edge to edge, likewise the chosen filling to slices of Wonder bread, press slices together, slice diagonally, present on plate, probably melamine because children couldn't be trusted with anything breakable. The good china was reserved for company on the holidays. Paper plates were totally out of bounds for meals in-home; they were strictly relegated to picnics.

In the time it took me to complete my own sandwich and of which I had taken approximately three bites, my brothers had finished theirs' and asked for seconds. Accordingly, I set my partially eaten sandwich aside and began the sandwich-making ritual for the second time. At that precise moment, our father entered the dining room through its door onto the back porch. He had an immediate unimpeded view of us gathered around the kitchen table. Upon seeing us, his high forehead wrinkled upward into his grizzled hair, which sprang in crisp waves toward the crown of his head. His Maxwell House coffee-colored eyes slanted down towards the mid point of his lips, which his clenched jaw was pulling into a thin slash. His face darkened, like a threatening thunderhead, with rage.

"You selfish bitch!" he screamed at me. He slammed the door shut as punctuation to his expressed judgment. Whatever further words he uttered have melted to the nightside of memory. I only remember their central theme: that I had made a sandwich for myself and sat selfishly eating it in front of my hungry little brothers who were too young to be able to make their own. (Brad was four or five; David was six.) He probably also further added that, as the eldest and therefore as my family's designated little mother, I was held accountable for the well-being of my younger brothers.

I heard that so often it seems unlikely he would have skipped an opportunity to say it yet again.

My eyes filled with tears. I tried to prevent them from running down my rubescent cheeks. I don't know if I succeeded. There is no way I can convincingly describe how afraid of my father I was, both at that moment and for years afterwards. Therefore, I will only say that I was so terrified my hands were trembling. That is another detail I remember with painful acuity, how my fingers were shaking just as the whip-like branches of the weeping willow on our side lawn would have if caught in lonely confrontation against the brutal gale charging across the featureless southern Illinois fields at the dead end of February.

My verbal response to my father, if indeed I offered one, has been obliterated from memory. Most likely, I was too scared to even consider speaking although not too scared to recognize my situation as hopelessly indefensible. Thus, I didn't try to explain. I certainly didn't try to tell him that he was wrong, that he had misinterpreted the scenario. Words like that were construed as talking back, being a smart ass. Dad would have vaulted across the gap separating us and slapped the shit out of me. Actually, I must retract that last assertion. Mom was the slapper. Dad would have smacked me. That was his favorite threat and mode of dealing with the thankless brats that an unfair world and his Catholic wife had foisted upon him.

That is all I remember. I can't say what the weather was like, where Dad went or what he did after this encounter, whether I eventually consumed the remainder of my partially eaten sandwich, or if I washed and dried the dishes afterwards. I probably finished eating my sandwich. Whatever the circumstances, throwing food in the garbage was forbidden. And besides, I had to be mindful of the starving children in China who would have been grateful to eat anything I didn't want to eat. I probably washed, dried, and put away the dishes as well. I would have dreaded the consequences if I hadn't done so.

Nor can I bring to mind what my brothers did or said. They hadn't sprung to my defense, nor had I expected them to. In such situations, each one of us was accustomed to fall back into defensive, self-preservation mode. During that specific occurrence, David and Brad impersonated blind, deaf, and dumb – most definitely dumb – garden gnomes. If it were possible, they probably would have willed themselves to be two tiny dust motes in the darkest angle of our house's twelve-foot ceilings.

"Dad is wiping the walls with Judy, so, while he's distracted, I am hustling my scared and sorry ass out of here," they may well have thought as they considered how best to react. But I believe both they and I must have remained paralyzed in that tableau – exactly as, sixty years gone by, my memory has fixed us.

<hr />

My father bought himself a box of chocolate candy bars. Memory fails me here. I can't remember any more specifically than that what they were. Perhaps Clark bars or maybe Heath bars; I think Dad liked those. "These are mine," he announced to my brothers and me. At half his height, we were like scraggly garden weeds to the sunflower of his sovereign persona. He had gathered the four of us, ranging in age at that time from four to twelve, not to read us a children's fairy tale but to tell us this real world truth. "These candy bars are mine. Not yours. These are for me to eat, and you can't have any." And he meant that literally. He bought a whole box of chocolate candy bars for himself, and he had no intentions of sharing them. My brothers and I were not allowed to have any of them, not even one. That much I very specifically remember.

I don't remember, though, if Mom was also barred from eating them. I can't remember either if Mom pleaded with Dad to share his candy with his children. She may have spoken to him when they were alone together, but I don't know that either. She was so pressured by her belief that she needed to keep our old ten room house fastidiously clean and cook three daily meals for six from scratch that doling out candy bars wasn't a battle she felt inclined to join. I doubt that she told us behind his back, "It's OK. He didn't mean it like he made it sound. Go ahead and take one." If she had said that or something similar, we might have each taken and eaten one hoping that she would protect us thereafter from Dad's wrath, or that we could divert it by claiming, "But Mom said we could." But, truthfully, I don't remember her being involved in any way in the candy bars incident.

My brothers and I weren't surprised by Dad's behavior and edict. He was being true to himself, comporting himself totally within the parameters of his character as we grew up knowing it. I don't recall, in this particular instance, whether Dad also issued a specific consequence if we dared help ourselves to his candy. Dad depended on the implicit threat of his potential violence to guard everything he regarded as 'his', especially from us. Apparently, his children were not sufficiently 'his' to merit similar protection. When within range of his malefic surveillance we might bow, as all of us always did, to the impossibility of doing anything other than what he ordered. That didn't mean, however, that we were lacking a sweet tooth ourselves. Nor did it mean that we would be willing to forswear our desire to have a candy bar because our father was unwilling to share his cache.

If one of my brothers or I, however, had been the one with some treat or treasure which we didn't want to share with our siblings, a different set of rules was in force. Dad would have loudly, harshly castigated the miserly ankle-biter. And very likely called that child names and sworn at him or her. That's how we learned that we were undeserving little shits. If he were feeling particularly vexed, Dad would yank the treat or treasure away from the selfish one and either give it to one of our siblings or force us to watch him break it and throw it in the garbage. While he was at it, he would yell at us, "If you can't share, then you can't have any at all, you selfish little brat."

Dad put his box of chocolate candy bars on the top shelf in a kitchen cabinet. My brothers and I were conflicted. Our candy craving augmented by a nearly full box of it under our family roof tantalized us just as our craven fear of him taunted us. But Dad wasn't able to stand guard over his candy all day every day. At the first propitious moment of his absence from the house and when Mom was out of sight as well, David and I pushed a kitchen chair up to the cabinets. By standing on the chair, I was able to reach into the box of candy bars, and I removed four of them, one for myself as well as one for each of my three brothers.

We felt compelled to be sneaks, but not recklessly so. David and I had devised a plan prior to our even attempting the candy grab. We agreed that, if Dad noticed that the candy bars were missing, we would endeavor to stave off the anticipated punishment by expressing our readiness to pay for what we had taken. I suggested that I would offer to pay for Brad's and mine if David would pay for his and Gordon's. "It's a deal," David agreed.

Dad did notice. When he returned home, he counted the candy bars. I believe he ordered my brothers and me to come stand before him immediately in order to be confronted with his accusation of our thievery. And David and I just as quickly proposed to pay him for the purloined candy. Our pre-planned offer erupted from us faster than his upraised, work-hardened hand could fall upon any part of our unprotected little bodies. Our buyout proposal worked. David and I promptly produced our money and each of us handed our father one slim silver dime for the chocolate candy bars which we had stolen from him. I think Dad most likely swore at us and called us ungrateful little sneaks, but, just that once, his reprisals didn't escalate to their not-uncommon spasm of physical violence.

This incident occurred many years ago when our grandparents were still living in caves and hunting mastodons with stone axes to feed themselves. Which was also the last time chocolate candy bars cost five cents.

One warm day, Dad took David, Brad, and me to play at the fairgrounds located at the north end of Second Street. I definitely remember it being a sunny day in the late afternoon or early evening. None of us were wearing coats or sweaters, evidence of that day's warmth. Possibly it was summer because my brothers and I were not in school, or possibly it was a weekend because Dad was not at work. Many other particulars of that day are sunk so deep in the quicksand of my memory as to be unrecoverable. But I don't feel impelled to insert simulacra into the opaque lacunae.

The fragments of my remembrances are sufficient because they are significant.

I also distinctly recall that Mom was not with us. Typically she was always with us, but where she was that particular day I cannot even guess. It was unusual for Dad to be taking us anywhere without her. We were equally unlikely to be alone with our father outside of our house except, maybe, in the barn, corn-crib, or brooder house. It was not like him to even escort us off our fourteen-acre property to any place other than his parent's home. I can't say why Dad took the initiative to bring us any place such as he did that afternoon. Maybe our mother had suggested he take us out. Maybe he wanted to give her a break from her twenty-four hour days of childcare duties, although it's practically impossible for me to imagine him possessing that much empathy. Gender roles were more inflexible at that time, and men did not provide childcare. I can't recollect it being mentioned, but perhaps he was finding us too noisy to be tolerated within the confines of "his castle," so we were being herded out into a larger arena that would better absorb our rambunctious uproar.

The fairgrounds were so named because every year the Clark County Fair was held at that location. The fairgrounds possessed two horse barns and a dirt racetrack with stands for spectators. Harness races, the common man's horse racing sport, were offered in the afternoons during the fair. Interspersed with the Standardbred trotters and pacers pulling a two-wheeled cart called a sulky, were a few of what we called flat or running races, horses racing under saddle. Usually a few horses were stabled and trained at the fairgrounds throughout all but the coldest months of the year.

Closer to the short road leading into the fairgrounds and a stone's throw from the stables and track was a cluster of playground equipment. It was nothing fancy. The sturdy merry-go-round, slide, and swings were scattered on non-manicured grass that was beaten down to the underlying dirt in areas with the most foot traffic. Nearby was a drinking fountain. It wasn't fancy either but rather a rudimentary contraption consisting of a standpipe, faucet, and trough fashioned from wood planks.

My brothers and I may have wished we had brought a sheet of wax paper with us that afternoon to use on the slide. Dad would have never allowed us to do that, of course. That would be wasteful and that's not what wax paper was for anyway. But sometimes some of our playmates did bring a piece of wax paper when they played there. You could sit on the wax paper to shoot down the slide faster than otherwise possible. And it left the metal surface of the slide slicker for at least a short interval.

I don't know how my brothers and I entertained ourselves that particular afternoon. We didn't do anything out of the ordinary that I can recall. I doubt that we checked out what was happening at the racetrack or horse barns. If Dad brought us to the fairgrounds to play on the swings and other apparatus, we were restricted to doing exactly that. Why have an agenda if it wasn't going to be adhered to? So, I assume we did what we and our cousins and friends usually did there.

We swung on the swings leaning our whole body alternately way back and then way forward to pump ourselves as high into the sky as we possibly could. We jointly pushed the merry-go-round, running around its circumference, then at the agreed upon signal, we all jumped on it together to ride until its spinning momentum dissipated. We tried to climb up the slide from the bottom end as well as using the ladder to reach the top. We opened the faucet on the fountain, not only to drink the water, but also in an attempt to spray each other by occluding part of the water outlet with a thumb. We took care while we were at it not to step into the muddy puddle forming at the base of the fountain.

To my brothers and me it seemed we were at the fairgrounds for only a short time when Dad suddenly shouted at us, "All right, that does it. You're going straight home and straight to bed when we get there."

"Why? What did we do?" we had the impudence to ask.

"You know."

I can recall perfectly well that we most emphatically did not know. We had no idea. This was not an unusual predicament for us. We often found ourselves subjected to impossible-to-understand accusations and arbitrary punishments. But our father expected us to always know his murky rules of proper behavior for children, perhaps by osmosis. We didn't argue. We remained mute. It was sad enough to be ordered into the house and into bed before the sun had set and made worse because it was for no reason that we could fathom. But if we put forward any more questions or arguments, he would smack us. Smack -- that was one of his favorite words and threats when he spoke to us. I don't believe we held conversations with him. He barked orders; we complied, silently if we knew what was good for us.

In cheerless single file, with me in the lead followed by David, then Brad, and with Dad at the tail end, he herded us along the roadway of crushed white stone from the fairgrounds up to Second Street. We were baffled. What might we have done to displease him this time? Was it because we tried to spin the merry-go-round fast enough to make ourselves sick to our stomachs while riding it? Or was he irked that, when the swing reached the apogee of its arc, we loosed our hold on it and launched ourselves into a five second competition with gravity? Perhaps he was peeved that we tried to scramble up the dented, silvery slide like heathens instead of utilizing the climbing ladder. "If there's a ladder attached to something, it's there for a reason," Dad had informed us I'm sure. Did we infuriate him by inadvertently stepping in a puddle under the water faucet thereby harming the shoes for which he paid good money?

Our procession trudged homeward along the narrow, bucking sidewalk of North Second Street past the few single-family homes strewn on idiosyncratically sized and shaped plots of land. Every home, ours included, featured an irregular collection of chairs and swings on its front porch or front yard. Their day's activities wrapped up, the inhabitants of all these residences actually settled in to sit a spell on what today we might call their lanai but back then were front porches. From there they called out neighborly greetings to passersby. And that was a good thing. If this personable citizenry had not been accustomed to so sitting and conversing, my younger brothers and I might have lived out our lives in ignorance of the transgression we had perpetrated that afternoon.

One of these good people, I can't say who, called out from a porch to our father. That someone might even have been his grandfather or Edith, who lived next door to us in a white house as tired in its decrepitude as our own. Nor do I remember exactly what that person said or asked. Dad's response, however, is one of those shards that cut through memory-dissolving time. He explained, "They're going home to bed because they were playing in the water."

Now, at last, our offense was revealed. But only because we over-heard one sentence he spoke to another adult. My brothers and I, not only didn't know until that moment what we had done wrong, we hadn't regarded our activities by the drinking fountain to be the despicable wrong of "playing in the water." We judged ourselves to have been engaged in the legitimate tasks of childhood: playing, by and with water in this instance, and bedeviling our siblings. Our father expanded no effort that afternoon – or any other morning, noon, or night either – to emend our misapprehensions whenever we chanced to fall short of his expectations. The only information he habitually dispensed to us in such situations was, "You know."

At this far remove in time, I can't remember whether we were ordered into bed when we reached home a few minutes after that casual adult interchange. But I do wonder if Dad ever wondered why his children persistently provoked his wrath and punishment by habitually misbehaving when he knew that our knowing and interpretation of right conduct was an exact replica of that which was secreted within his own mind.

⁂

Early one Sunday morning I pulled out a section of the news-paper, very likely the funnies. Dad noticed what I was reading and ordered me to put it back. "I want to read the Sunday paper before you God-damned brats mess it up," he yelled. I silently replaced whatever section I had been reading. My mother tried to say some-thing consoling to me about my father's need for orderliness and for getting first dibs. I cannot recall the words she used, only that she offered that gesture. I just nodded my head as I sidled through the dining room door to the back porch with my face averted, so Dad wouldn't see the tears in my eyes.

"God is like your father," Father C., a Jesuit priest at Loyola University informed me. As the good father was saying this, he wiggled his fleshy fingers into the crease between my torso and the top of my thigh in case the black and white checked skirt with flower appliques, which my grandmother had sewn for me, was, perchance, inadvertently trapped in my hip joint. Then he smoothed out any wrinkles that might have been incubating in the cotton fabric by running his warm moist hand, like a steam iron, along the material draped over my thigh and knee, after which he gave my skirt's hem a persuasive tug as if he were assuring himself that my kneecap was modestly covered.

"God forbid," I responded. "My father was a wife-beater and child-molester."

"That poor man. You should pray for him."

10

Family Secrets

CONCOMITANT WITH THE fifties-mandated family togetherness were family secrets. Growing up in the fifties required suppression and pretense. It was not all right to not love your family members or to not be happy.

Years after the fact, my mother declared, "Everyone knew Jackie (Uncle Lauf and Aunt Mary's third child and only son) wasn't Lauf's." Everyone didn't include me. Otherwise, this was apparently one of those family secrets that wasn't.

I once mentioned Betty. I realized she was connected in some way – and the only way I knew was marriage – to my Great-Uncle Dick, Gramma's brother. "We don't talk about Betty," Mammoo cautioned me. "She's your Uncle Dick's mistress."

David knew more of these family secrets and back-stories than I ever did. I must have passed through those same years in a daydream or deeply absorbed in a book. David, on the other hand, must have gone everywhere with his eyes and ears open but his head down. He was cheeky enough to be chuckled over as a little rascal but clever enough to avoid attracting too much attention to himself. In our home, attention, especially from the implacable authority of our father, was usually negative.

As David and I grew older, I tried to make myself appear to be extremely fond of him. I vaguely hoped that our mother's exaggerated affection for David would spill over onto me, the less favored satellite in his orbit. It didn't work. Instead, Mom tried to use any feeling I might have for David and the rest of my brothers against me. I should visit over the weekend because David would be home. Brad would be disappointed if I didn't attend some wedding. As youngsters, my siblings and I were encouraged to tattle on each other. Now Mom made it sound like the happiness of my siblings was dependent upon my physical presence at what she deemed momentous events.

※

One evening I was alone in the house with Dad. That was rare. Although he preferred to spend his evenings at home watching his television, or reading his comic books or his copy of Marshall's daily newspaper, he did not appreciate the rest of his family disturbing him when he was engaged in his personal pursuits. Dad wasn't fond of the company of his children. He didn't insert himself into our activities, except to threaten to smack us if we didn't keep quiet. He was even disinclined to help us with our homework. For my part, I avoided my father as much as possible or, failing that, tried to fade into the wallpaper when we chanced to be in the same room. I didn't like him and I didn't trust him. He might lash out at any time, ridiculing us, shouting threats or insults, or striking us. If the strength of a punch from him knocked my brothers or me down, he would kick us until we managed to scramble up or to crawl out of his reach. But that specific night, for some now unremembered reason, I chose to seat myself in an armchair in the front room in front of the TV. I don't recall if it was even on. Since it wasn't yet my bedtime, it may be that my brothers had already gone to bed, so I wouldn't have been allowed to disturb them by remaining in our common bedroom.

Decades before the concept of helicopter parents emerged, my mother seemed to police my own and my brothers' activities more closely than did the parents of our friends. Perhaps, that was because she had been born and raised in Chicago and had survived eighteen years of being cautioned by her own mother about strangers enticing her with bags of penny candy and offers of rides to Hell in their souped-up jalopies. But she was absent that particular evening.

Even though she had eyes in the back of her head, my mother couldn't see through time like Paul Muad'Dib Atreides, protagonist of Frank Herbert's *Dune* chronicles. And even though she had the energy of the uncontrollable forces of nature, my mother wilted incrementally in her face-off with the social expectations placed on women in the fifties. Realistically she quite simply couldn't be in all places at all times or see everything that all of us were doing. Thus, my ability to achieve a limited level of safety in her shadow was imperfect and progressively compromised.

So that night I was sitting in that armchair. The tall windows of the front room had evolved into black panels, evidence that the sun was well below the horizon. Then Dad appeared and sat down on me. I don't know where he was previously. I only remember the shocking suddenness of his physical body pinning me into the armchair. I couldn't slide myself sideways out from under him because of the chair arms. He was so much heavier than I was that I couldn't simply force him off my lap by standing up. I was afraid of him in routine situations; now I was too terrified to try to muscle him off of me, to beg him to get off of me, or to cry out for someone else's help.

I almost felt more a sense of disturbed surprise than fear because I didn't understand why he was doing this to me. He didn't explain himself or hint that this was his idea of a joke. He said little or nothing to me, no single thing that I can remember with certitude. He wasn't laughing as if he were roughhousing with me. I was too intimidated to put my palms on his back and try to push him off my thighs. I didn't have enough strength to do so anyway. I could barely think of what to say or do. I was crippled by panicky incomprehension.

I can't say how long he remained sitting on me. It was an extended period of time, sufficient for the weight and heat of his buttocks and thighs to press wrinkles into the blue corduroy skirt I was wearing. When, how, or why he released me has fled my remembrance. I haven't the slightest recollection how that night ended. Whether from embarrassment or fear of not being believed, or my intuitive understanding that I would never win redress for any harm my father inflicted on me, I never mentioned this incident to Mom or anyone else.

My parents must have been enjoying an evening out because I had been bedded down in their bedroom on the first floor. Still a toddler, Gordon slept in a crib at the foot of their bed. They probably didn't want to leave him alone in the otherwise empty ground level of the house. I presume that David and Brad were sleeping in their shared bedroom on the second floor. When Mom and Dad returned, they rousted me out of their bed, so I could finish the night sleeping in my own bed on the second floor.

Dad, walking behind me with his hands on my waist, propelled me like a sleepwalker over to the stairway. I don't know where Mom had gone. Perhaps to the bathroom or to check on Gordon. Wherever she was, she was not any place where I could see her. As we approached the first turn of the staircase, Dad reached under my pajama top and cupped the warm fingers of his right hand over the fatty little tumor that passed for my right breast. His maneuver could not have been an accidental innocent contact. Metaphorically I felt as though some mythic deity had smote me with the lightning bolt of retributive destruction. I was shocked, panicked, so alarmed that I caught my toes on the lip of the next riser. As I stumbled, I burned my left forearm on the lit cigarette Dad was holding in his left hand. He immediately pulled his left hand away and gripped my right wrist with his right hand as if he were trying to protect me, both from falling and from burning myself on his cigarette.

I remember nothing past that instant. Every further moment of that night is unavailable to my recall; all else has passed behind the opaque veil where memories transit to evaporate. That stealthy groping increased the fear and hatred I felt towards my father. As usual I didn't tell my mother. I felt so humiliated that informing anyone else seemed likely to exacerbate my shame. Even worse, what if I wasn't believed? Nobody had to tell me that my father was selfish, violent, and a hypocritical sneak. He proved that much every week. I didn't want to believe his intimidations would become sexualized. Nor could I think of anybody who would want to believe this was happening in our white working class family, a family that had been resident in the area since before the city of Marshall was founded.

Dad was in receipt of much good will as the son of the well known and highly regarded O.B. and the grandson of local entrepreneur Pop. Dad had not inherited Pappy and Pop's outgoing personalities. He was reticent but put forward a pleasing public persona. Like a cliché of the most accommodating hostess, Dad would listen to other adults with an ingratiating grin on his face, periodically nodding or shaking his head, and intermittently uttering an American variation like, "Oh, boy," of the "Ah so" supposedly uttered by obsequious Japanese women. He never told any of these other adults that nobody had asked for their opinion as he had done to me. He never threatened to smack them. He never told them they were lazy, selfish, or ungrateful little shits. Dad prepared a public face to meet the faces of the adults who could hurt him back. He could and did set that mask aside when he was behind his closed castle doors. I had no confidence that any other adult would believe me if I tried to describe Dad in a way that varied from the public performances that they witnessed.

Sometimes a worse conjecture troubled me. From time to time, such as when she gifted me with red polyester see-through pajamas for Christmas, I believed that my mother did know that Dad's abuse had escalated from physical and emotional to sexual, but she chose not to acknowledge it. She could avoid having to deal with what she avoided knowing. It was like the magical thinking underpinning her "because I said so" reasons to control my behavior. I could never be harmed by what she never clarified. Realistically though, even if I had told my mother, even if she believed me, she and, therefore, I as well, would have had no remedy. Dad was our sole means of support. If he were removed from our lives at that time, my mother with four children under the age of twelve would have been helpless in the fullest sense of that word. Pappoo and Mammoo would have been unable and unwilling to take us in. I became hyper-vigilant, easily startled and sleepless at night, cringing when people touched me or stood behind me. I tried never to let Dad get within arm's reach of me. But I kept my mouth shut and put on my fifties happy family mask to face the world.

When I was fourteen and our family of seven was shoe-horned into a four room basement apartment in Chicago, Dad's predations escalated. But the pattern was set. I maintained the silence and the pretense until I could find a means of escape. That, however, is a different story of a different place.

11

What I Learned from My Father

1. No one wants to hear from me.

2. My middle name is Buttinsky and no one asked for my opinion.

3. My ass is fat and lazy.

4. Big people physically, emotionally, and sexually abuse people who are smaller and weaker than themselves because they can, and that's OK because that's a big people prerogative.

5. He doesn't ever have to tell me how he expects me to behave because I KNOW (his rules that are hidden deep within the darkest, most secret recesses of his mind.) [But sometimes telepathy simply doesn't function as well as he believed it did.]

6. He doesn't have to tell me what I did wrong because I KNOW (what I did wrong). [See No. 5 above. Ditto for osmosis.]

7. I have to do or refrain from doing, or can have or can not have something because he said so, that's why.

8. Disagreement is banned.

Words lost their meaning, and I lost my voice because Dad's opinion was the only correct one. I stopped speaking because the voice in my head replaced the voice of my father, and it kept telling me that no one was interested in anything I might say. I came to believe that I could express myself better in writing. Writing was something I could perform cautiously, revise often, and keep secret.

12

From the Land to the Dinner Table

TO THE ADHERENTS of the recently emerging locavore and slow food movements, our circumstances in Marshall must appear to have been idyllic. We did not employ insecticides, herbicides, or fertilizer on any of the vegetation on our land. I have no knowledge of what the area farmers applied to their commercial crops, but I imagine that whatever they used, if anything, was in more moderate doses than modern factory farms must utilize. We were wholly ignorant of the current notion of farmers markets like those that have sprouted in Chicago's loop and neighborhoods, and of community supported agriculture (CSA) in which customers support small scale, usually family farms, by purchasing shares of a farm's output.

Even those of us who lived in town usually maintained vegetable and flower gardens, and we were willing to share and swap with our relatives and neighbors. Rather than haul their produce into designated areas of the nearest cities or solicit a network of share holders, farmers who were so inclined set up wooden stands alongside the road in the vicinity of their houses from which to sell their produce or simply positioned a sign against a fence or on a post announcing what they had on offer. Farmers and customers relied on word of mouth instead of the Internet to find each other, but we thought we were managing just fine.

In Marshall there really was a spring, an interlude during which the florae surrounding us exhibited a delicate green tinge. And every spring we sowed tomatoes, sweet corn, string beans, carrots, radishes, and potatoes in a plot of land behind our house. I will speak of the corn later because corn and soybean fields are all but synonymous with southern Illinois. Our fourteen acres of land also included five varieties of mature fruit trees. Wild berries sequestered in the remnants of the tallgrass prairie. Come harvest time, Mom, often with Mammoo's assistance, canned tomatoes and summer fruits.

We planted potatoes that hadn't been eaten soon enough, those whose eyes had begun to sprout. We cut apart the potatoes so that each section contained a sprouted eye, which we then entrusted to furrows in the garden soil. When the potato plants matured, we unearthed them with a pitchfork. Potatoes that were inadvertently speared by the pitchfork tines didn't go to waste. We heaved them into the pig lot to be eaten by our hogs. My mother sometimes scrubbed the potato skins and ate them. My siblings and I thought she was crazy. Everyone knew that potato peels were meant for pigs to consume not people. We grew carrots, radishes, and occasionally lettuce from seeds. My brothers and I tried to gauge how fast our radishes and carrots were developing by scratching away the dirt with our fingers when their feathery green tops shouldered their way through the surface soil. Afterwards, we patted the dirt back up against the immature red or orange globes until the next time we checked their progress a day or two later.

One summer my father raised what we called muskmelons but which in Chicago are commonly known as cantaloupes. He planted a patch of them on the plateau of land west of or behind the barn. The muskmelons of his resulting crop were relatively small in size, about the circumference of a softball. Despite that, I heard that they tasted good. I have no empirical evidence to confirm that report. Dad wouldn't let the rest of us eat them. He told my brothers and me flat out, "You can't have any."

With the warming temperatures, a line of rhubarb stalks and asparagus shoots made their yearly appearance between our vegetable garden and the flagstone path that led from the grassy patch of our backyard to the barbed wire fence of the big pig lot. Dad had unearthed this path the year we moved into the old Montgomery house. Mom was the only one of us who appreciated asparagus, so the minimal number of them that ripened in intermittent waves was just the right amount. My brothers and I didn't favor rhubarb either but could be cajoled into eating it if it was cooked with sugar – lots of sugar. My mother also combined cooked, sugared rhubarb with store-bought strawberries for a fruit dessert for us. Preparing strawberry-rhubarb pie was too much effort though for something Dad was not likely to eat.

As our uncultivated fields baked in the oven of a southern Illinois July and August, we could smell the wild strawberries that sprouted in the tall grass and brambles. But they were too small and few in number to justify foraging for. So we bought strawberries from the farmers whose fields flourished with them. David, Brad and I did, however, expend sweaty hours and risked scratched arms and legs with Mom and Mammoo picking the raspberries and blackberries that grew in the same locations. We younger pickers probably ate half as many as survived for later family enjoyment, as strawberries were, with Bisquick biscuits and whipped cream. Our family almost never bought the commercial shortcakes intended for strawberries. They were an unnecessary extravagance easily replaced by Bisquick, that 1930s multi-use mix which was a staple in my mother and grandmother's pantries.

We never ate the fruit from the trees on our property. She had been born and raised in Chicago, so my mother was highly suspicious of fresh fruit that didn't grow on grocery store shelves. It didn't help either that we never applied pesticide to our trees. As a result, the appearance of their fruit was never uniformly flawless. The apricots looked the most unappetizing, shriveled like the tree upon which they grew and speckled with dark blemishes. The cherries were a tart variety that the birds appreciated more than we did. Our feathered friends stripped the cherries from the trees as fast as they ripened, then pooped red excreta onto whatever we had hanging on the clothes lines. (We didn't have a clothes dryer.) Giving my mother one more reason to dislike both those cherries and Marshall.

Two red apple trees, of a variety unknown to me then and now, grew in the big pig lot. They too were often marred with black spots. When the apples fell or were knocked off the trees by us, the pigs ate them. One aged pear tree grew behind our garage. Since we didn't pick and eat the pears either, they finally released their grip on the boughs when they matured to overripe. They lay rotting on the ground where they fell, exuding an aroma that attracted bees and hornets. We tip-toed around them to reach our swing set, which sheltered under the pear tree's limbs. As summer progressed, we played there cautiously, if at all. Periodically Mom or Dad, with our help, pulled out the wheelbarrow. We scooped the disintegrating fruits into the wheelbarrow, which we then rolled down to our hog enclosures where we up-ended the fragrant puree into the pig troughs.

Within the bed of lilies-of-the-valley that arced out in a semi-circle into our northern side yard grew two Pawpaw trees with their long drooping dark-green obovate leaves. Pawpaws, also spelled papaw, are a member of the custard apple family indigenous to the United States. Despite that, I had never seen such trees before, nor have I seen them anywhere else since then. The trees produce clusters of oblong yellow fruit containing two rows of one to one-and-a-half inch long, brownish to blackish seeds shaped like lima beans. The largest Pawpaws resemble plump mangoes. The ripe fruit is soft, thin-skinned and very perishable, which may be the reason Pawpaws don't appear in Chicago's grocery stores.

I'm sure the Pawpaws were unfamiliar to my mother as well. She refused to eat their fruit, as did I. I wouldn't even taste it when Pappy peeled and sliced one. Pappy was willing to eat them, and David sampled a bite. I found something off-putting about their mottled greenish to yellowish skin, dull gold fruit, and pronounced perfumey fragrance. Like the pears, we also fished the pulpy, elongated, decaying ovals of the Pawpaws from amongst the delicate white bell-shaped lilies-of-the-valley and conveyed them in a wheelbarrow down to the hog lot.

I don't think that we had mulberry trees on our property, but we were familiar with them because they grew elsewhere in Marshall. During my many years living in Chicago, I have seen exactly one mulberry tree. It was on North Dearborn Street in the Gold Coast neighborhood before its removal several years ago. Mulberry trees have a distinctive profile with crowns nearly equal to their height, and bark displaying long ridges and vertical cracks or furrows. You often find as many as three differently shaped leaves on the same tree: oval, mitten-like, and with at least three separate lobes. They are also distinguishable, particularly if near sidewalks, because of the dusky circular stain around their base as the ripe fruit drops from its slender stalk to decay or be trampled under foot.

The mulberries themselves are long, oval-shaped aggregate fruits composed of many berries stuck together, each with its own seed. The berries, red when unripe, darken to black with a reddish undertone when ripe. Even in a refrigerator, the ripe berries last only a few days. They ferment or become moldy because of their high water content and thin skin. That explains ripe mulberries unavailability in grocery stores, although I have seen dried mulberries at a Whole Foods Market. Like the Pawpaws, I never tasted the mulberries either. Since my mother turned up her nose in disgust and declared, "I don't care what Pappy said. Those may be poisonous," I likewise feared eating them.

We had elderberry bushes bunched in our big pig lot. Although they are indigenous flora, I have never seen them anywhere except in Marshall. The spherical, black to blue-black berries are tiny, about one-eighth of an inch across, and juicy and grow in branched clusters. Elderberries frequently appear in European wines, cordials, and jellies. Some people also regard them as possibly effective against flu symptoms. Cooked, the berries are considered safe, but when raw or unripe they might cause nausea, vomiting, or diarrhea. So perhaps it's just as well that we never ate the elderberries either. Pappy described to David and me how to brew elderberry wine. Following his directions, we produced at least one or two Mason jars of hazardous appearing liquid – which we were afraid to drink.

We did eat most of the vegetables we grew. The somewhat narrow range of our garden produce didn't matter. Dad's range of food preferences was comparably narrow and, if he didn't like certain foodstuffs, they were never served at our table. He favored green beans, peas, and carrots. Although he had no teeth and wore a full set of upper and lower dentures, he would eat corn on the cob, too. Mashed potatoes with gravy were a given; Mom served them, in addition to a vegetable, at supper every day. Fifties meal conventions commanded that supper consist of meat, potatoes and a vegetable. Serving plates of Wonder bread and butter (usually in our case the less expensive oleomargarine) were also dutifully set out on the supper table. At the end of the meal, the uneaten slices of bread were returned to their wrapper. The stick of butter substitute remained on the table, was removed to a kitchen counter, or was tucked into a kitchen cupboard because Dad preferred it soft. Margarine, cold and hard from the refrigerator, tore the bread apart instead of spreading smoothly across it.

I don't remember whether Dad also ate the cooked spinach and lima beans Mom periodically served. David and I did notice that Dad would sometimes pass around a serving bowl of food but not put any of it on his own plate. We didn't call attention to that because we knew what was good for us. And I don't mean that we knew Dad was depriving himself of the delicious and nutritious food Mom spent hours in a hot kitchen preparing for us with her own loving hands. Dad had already frequently warned us, "the only reason for you to open your mouth at the dinner table is to put food in it, if you know what's good for you."

My brothers and I were not allowed to leave the table or have dessert unless we ate everything on our plates. Once, when David and I were seated separately at a small table near a window, we tried hiding the food we didn't like behind the window curtains. We didn't get away with it. Much later, when the rejected food was found, Dad forced us to stand before him and eat it, cold and dirty as it was.

After I had left home, David related the following story to me. "Dad ordered Brad to eat the Brussels sprouts that were put on his plate even though Brad said he didn't like them. But you can't get away with saying that to Dad, so Brad ate them. Then he threw up all over the table. Since then Dad has stopped ordering us to eat food that we don't like." David and I agreed, "I wish we'd thought of that years sooner."

It may seem like we resided in the kingdom of organic home grown or family farmed fruits and vegetables, but our hogs ate more of the fruit our land produced than we did. And as my former sister-in-law noted, "Back then there were only two ways to cook anything. If it was meat, you fried it to death. If it was a vegetable, you boiled it to death."

Invariably our vegetables had been harvested within the twenty-four hours prior to our eating them. But my mother was not a woman to swim against the tide. She boiled every vegetable down to a flaccid state, then poured the water, including the water soluble vitamins and minerals leached out by the boiling process as nutritionists now warn us, down the drain and stirred up to a stick of margarine into the pot. After that, she dirtied another dish by scraping the slick limp vegetables into a serving bowl. Despite all that, I remember that they tasted delicious. They were better by far than the insipid green slush then passing for vegetables that we encountered upon our return to Chicago.

13

Southern Illinois = Corn Fields

IN PLANTING OUR sweet corn, we adhered to tradition. Punch a hole in Illinois' dark prairie dirt with a triangular-shaped hand trowel or, alternatively, create a shallow furrow with a long-handled hoe, drop in four corn kernels and I forget how many string bean seeds a foot apart, then pack a loose mound of dirt over the seed mix by hand or by means of the hoe. A farmer's formula explained the four corn kernels: one for the earth, one for the crow, one for the worm, and one to grow. The vines of the green beans wrapped themselves around the ripening corn stalks so that the beans were pulled heavenward up off the ground by the corn stalks as they stretched toward the sun.

In our garden between the house and big pig lot, we planted sweet corn for our own consumption. In the larger field by the barn and corn-crib, we planted what was called field corn for the pigs. Living in Chicago years later, a younger female acquaintance responded with considerable irritation when I mentioned this. She had never been made aware that people and livestock don't eat the same corn. I concluded that she was another one of those people who believe that incidents, items, ideas, and details of which they have no personal knowledge or experience don't exist. This must so unbalance their equanimity that their instinctive response is to lash out in anger. Another woman of my acquaintance who was originally from Cardiff, Wales, told me that no one in Great Britain ate corn before World War II. Until their close contact with U.S. military personnel during that war, they had regarded corn as livestock fodder.

The old farmer's adage was that the corn stalks should be knee high by the Fourth of July. David and I always checked. As the summer wore on and the corn plants shot up over our head, we assessed the kernels' readiness. Pappy demonstrated the best method to use. He showed us how to peel back the tip of a husk to reveal the kernels budding at the tip of the cob. If the tip is not filled to its end with plump yellow or white kernels, that cob has more growing to do. Overripe sweet corn kernels, on the other hand, reveal slight indentations on their top edge. Next, you press your thumbnail into a kernel. On an ear that is ripe but not past its prime, the kernel will pop like a pustule, spitting out droplets of liquid and a bit of its soft white interior, or endosperm. That ear is ready to be picked and shucked, boiled or grilled, and eaten. In fact, it can be eaten "raw" immediately if picked at the optimal time.

By the time we moved away from Marshall, I could easily identify decent corn on the cob. I discovered, however, that many people in the Chicago area couldn't and happily ate tough corn on the cob whose sweetness had been aged and/or boiled out of it. Sweet corn is picked while the endosperm is in its milk stage, in other words while it is immature, and prepared and eaten as a vegetable rather than as a grain. Field corn is harvested when the kernels are dry and mature. In sweet corn, the process of maturation converts its sugar to starch. In Marshall, we were able to pick ears of corn at their peak and eat them the same day. By the time those same ears might have traveled to Chicago and sat on your grocer's shelf for three days, their sweet sugar was converted to starch.

Of course, part of growing and picking your own corn was husking it. That was a laborious process, pulling off every husk and filamentous silk tassel. If you weren't scrupulous, tender slivers of overlooked husk and strands of silk snagged between your teeth. That was a problem for Dad. And whatever made Dad unhappy became a problem for everyone in his vicinity because we were subjected to his sulking and griping. Careful attention also had to be paid to boiling the ears of corn. Leaving them overlong in the boiling water rendered them as tough as leaving them on the stalk too long.

The adults around us were able to keep us on task preparing the ears of corn by reminding us of our goal: eating clean, perfectly delicious, and deliciously sweet corn on the cob slathered with butter and crusted with salt. Some of us will swear those are two of the three major food groups, fat and salt, chocolate being the third. Pappy also taught us the best method for buttering an ear of corn. Lavishly butter a slice of bread, then wrap the bread around the ear of corn with one hand and, holding one end of the corn with the other hand, slide the buttered bread up and down the ear. This worked well for young children with clumsy fingers. The only drawbacks were the slices of buttered bread, which, of course, we never wanted to eat afterwards. If none of the adults ate them for us, they were delegated to the pigs. If we were at Pappy and Gramma's, the unwanted bread slices along with the corn cobs ended up in Gramma's compost pile, an unpretentious mound of discarded table scraps, egg shells, coffee grounds and grass clippings at the far end of their backyard. Most of us had similar sites on our own property for organic refuse. This was years before I had ever heard of composting bins; and worm bins, farms, and factories. Modest and informal though they were, the compost piles of Marshall seemed to work quite satisfactorily. If we were lacking, we were cheerful in our ignorance of our deficits.

Although we didn't plant them, there were also many acres around Marshall given over to soybeans. At that time, I had no idea what they were or what was done with them. My mother had some vague understanding that they served as animal fodder. Neither one of us connected soybeans to the Kikkoman soy sauce we splashed on Mom's pseudo-Chinese Chop Suey. Nor did we know that tofu or tempeh even existed. I should have asked our Chautauqua preceptor Pappy. Having said that, even he couldn't have foretold the explosion of soy-based products consumed today by non-Asian Americans. Now even the lactose-intolerant can stand in line with the rest of us for their five-dollar soy lattes at Starbucks.

14

From the Barnyard to the Dinner Table

OUR FAMILY LIVED within the city limits as did our next-door neighbors Pop and Edith. In farm country, our properties were not considered farms despite our livestock and various out-buildings. As for the chickens and pigs that filled our chicken yard and pigsties, we raised them to send to market.

On at least one occasion, I accompanied my mother to the farm supply store to buy a flat square box of downy chicks. We tumbled the chicks out of the box onto the brooder house floor where they clustered in a seething, chirping, yellow dot under a heat lamp suspended from the ceiling until feathers replaced their down. All chickens in Marshall were free-range chickens. Laying hens were not confined to battery cages. They were kept out of the elements in hen or brooder houses, which is what we had, with free access to an outdoor chicken yard. Although ours didn't, hen and brooder houses often had boxes or rails for the roosting hens. Neither we nor anyone else I can think of debeaked, or trimmed the beak of, laying hens. Debeaking implies the entire beak is removed, but, in fact, only one-half or less of it is trimmed.

Then, nobody considered their chickens to be pets, nor did anyone allow chickens into their homes. And we certainly did not put diapers on our chickens, which some people must be doing with what they apparently regard as their feathered friends, because several online businesses have washable cloth diapers on offer for chickens. Additionally, the October 10, 2013 issue of Chicago's alternative free weekly paper of news, politics, art, and culture, the *Chicago Reader*, featured a character sketch of a Chicago area chicken consultant. This young lady advises city dwellers on the care and upkeep of chickens. I always forward such articles to David with the question, "What is wrong with these people?" Chickens are livestock not pets, and they're certainly not family members..

We kept three Chester White sows, which Dad bred every year. He retained the sows but sold their offspring, who as shoats were trucked to the slaughterhouses in Chicago. We did not employ either gestation stalls (also known as sow stalls) or farrowing crates. Gestation stalls are enclosures used in intensive pig farming, a euphemism for factory farming. The size of the sow forms the basis for the dimensions of the stall, but they are too narrow to allow the animal to turn around. Commercially made ones are usually metal, and the floors are made of slatted concrete over a cesspool. Their defenders claim such stalls protect the sows from each other. In large groups, they will fight to establish dominance and to control the food supply.

Slightly before or after farrowing, the sows and their piglets are moved to farrowing crates that are slightly wider to enable the sow to lie down to nurse her litter. These crates have eighteen-inch troughs, or escape areas, on either side where the piglets can safely lay down without danger of being overlain by the sow. The sows are still so close to being immobilized that they often develop bedsores. Our own sows were housed, and farrowed in what may previously have been two equine box stalls in our barn, so these accommodations were quite roomy. Each of the stalls also had an entry to its own modestly-sized pigsty. An escape area for the piglets was created by nailing something like a low wood fence with widely spaced slats around the perimeter of the stalls. David claims that he helped Dad deliver a litter of piglets, which the sow killed and ate before Dad and David could even dry them off. This story strikes me as evidence of either David's imagination in action or his favored status as our parents' first-born son.

My parents did bring one of the piglets into the house to try to care for it after a sow stepped on it, putting a long gash across its ribs. I don't think it occurred to them to call a vet. The only time a vet might see our pigs was to castrate the newborn males. A farmer could probably accomplish that himself with a sharp knife, steady hands, and great intestinal fortitude. I'm assuming, of course, that a pig farmer is conversant with swine anatomy. We installed rings in our sows' noses. Unlike rings in cows' noses that pierce the septum, those in pigs' noses are open copper wire rings clipped to the rim of the nose. Their purpose is to prevent pigs from digging up or rooting in their enclosures, a natural behavior they engage in with their snouts. A rung pig is still able to forage freely through leaf mold and surface vegetation.

We had a red Duroc boar named Rodney, but only briefly. Boars had to be housed and fed but were of little use except for breeding. Pop and Edith owned a comparable number of sows. At least once, Edith asked Dad if his boar could cover her sows. When he agreed, she drove her sows across our adjoining yards on foot to our boar's pen, moving them along with a switch cut from a weeping willow tree. It goes without saying,,we were not managing a factory farm. I'm not aware of any in existence around us at that time. True to one stereotype of country bumpkins, though, we did stand on the pigsty fence, bang on a metal feed bucket (probably with a corn cob), and call the pigs up to the barn by shouting, "soo pig, sooey pig." A useful skill in the appropriate environment but not one I list on my resume.

We once owned a white-faced Hereford heifer. I believe we named her Elsie or Gladys, an appropriate sounding name for a heifer. I don't remember how she came into our lives nor her fate when she disappeared. I can make a good guess as to what became of her. White-faced Herefords are beef cattle common to south-central Illinois. So, she was essentially hamburger on the hoof. What I haven't forgotten though is that she was an excellent jumper. We tried to confine her to the small holding pens adjacent to the barn or to the big pig lot, but she sailed over our few wood and our long lines of barbed wire fences with the ease and grace of a gazelle. It was probably easier to speedily sell her to a butcher than worry about keeping track of and possibly losing her and the income she represented.

My father and his Uncle Lauf were engaged in the wholesale poultry and egg business. Uncle Lauf took over this business when his father Benjamin, otherwise known as Pop, decided, at the age of 74, to retire. Uncle Lauf's given name was Frank Laufman, his name derived from his mother's maiden name Ruth Ettie Laufman. We knew her as Mom. Uncle Lauf was Pappy's youngest brother and Pop and Mom's eighth child and sixth son. Dad and Uncle Lauf collected pullets, eggs, and 10-gallon cylindrical metal cans filled with raw cow's milk from the farmers in the surrounding countryside. One or two days a week in the very early morning they conveyed what they had gathered into Indianapolis or to the Water Street market in Chicago to sell to commercial merchants. Dad favored driving the pullets into Chicago on rainy days. He stacked the slatted chicken coops on an open flat bed truck for the nearly two hundred-mile trip. He could have covered them with a tarp but didn't. By the time he arrived at the market, the rain would have saturated the chicken's feathers so that they weighed more. Chickens sold by weight not by unit.

We never killed these animals ourselves for our own consumption. Even in my imagination, I can't assemble a picture of Mom laying one of her work weary hands upon a living, struggling animal and slitting its throat. Mammoo, however, when she visited us was not so squeamish. She was capable of cutting the chickens' throats and hanging them by their leathery yellow legs to bleed out while their bodies continued to twitch and their wings to flap.

Our elderly neighbor Mrs. McNary was not squeamish either about adding a fresh-killed chicken to the pot. However, she used a different, more gruesome, method. She would stretch the chicken's neck out along the ground, place the sturdy handle of a hoe over its neck, then plant both of her feet on the handle and pull the chicken towards her by its feet until its head ripped off. My brothers and I watched horrified, but fascinated, as the chicken's decapitated body flopped around on the ground for several moments more.

The labor didn't end when the chicken's still body signaled it was definitively dead. Mammoo and my mother had to rip out the feathers. I remember them standing at the gas stove burning the pinfeathers off the dimpled, yellowish-white chicken skin in the flames of the lit burners. After that the carcass still had to be gutted and dissected before it began to resemble the plastic wrapped chicken on Styrofoam trays available from chain grocery stores. Lastly the bird was fried, skin-on, in several inches of Crisco in a frying pan on the stove.

Despite a back yard filled with pigs and chickens and living in close proximity to cattle farms, we bought thin bone-in pork chops and ground beef at the store, and chicken as well when Mammoo wasn't visiting us. It seemed like we ate fried chicken every other night. The nights we didn't eat chicken we ate fried pork chops. Of course, we didn't really; it just seemed like we did. About once a year, Mom splurged and fixed a thin skirt steak. Even that was fried. On Fridays Mom served frozen fish sticks, frozen white fish, or tuna noodle casserole. Because of this, some of my childhood friends thought we must be Catholic. My mother was a lapsed Catholic, but when I asked her if that was why we ate fish on Friday she told me, "No. It's so we can have a change from eating meat every night."

Sundays were different, too. Mom habitually fixed a Sunday dinner of pot roast, potatoes, and carrots. She simmered the meat and vegetables on the stove's back burner for hours until the roast developed the taste and texture of a well-played football. Fortunately, gravy accompanied every Sunday dinner and weekday suppers, too. It helped abate the dryness of Mom's pot roast. It worked on her holiday turkey, also.

Occasionally, we hand churned into butter some of the milk that Dad and Uncle Lauf collected. I remember it as an arduous process. The milk had to be left in a shallow dish, which I have read were called pancheons (now a regional name in the United Kingdom), so the cream would rise to the top. Probably though, any shallow container would serve the purpose. The cream was skimmed off to churn. I'm sure my mother found some use for the skim milk that remained. If not in a recipe, then it was served to our swine. We used a glass paddle churn, which had a paddle inside attached to a rod turned by a handle either on the top or side of the churn. Ours resembled an oversize Mason canning jar, the lid fitted with a paddle inside and a turning handle on the outside. As we cranked the handle for what seemed like hours, we could see the butter coalescing on the paddles. My mother scraped it off the paddles and packed it into some kind of container. Such home churned butter didn't arise from the cream in sticks nor was it the deep yellow color associated with commercially made store-bought butter. My grandfather had to drink the buttermilk residue because no one else in the family could abide the taste of it. Either he drank it or it too was poured into the pig troughs.

I also remember savoring homemade ice cream while sitting with my family on the grass under the umbrella of the weeping willow's trailing branches as the dusk enveloped us. But no automatic ice cream maker with a heavy-duty motor that produces half a dozen frozen desserts within twenty minutes existed yet to produce our ice cream. We created it in similar fashion to the hand churned butter. Dad's role in the process was to fill the outer wooden bucket with ice and rock salt. Inside the bucket was a can, now usually stainless steel, and a dasher system inside of that. The dasher system was electroplated cast iron with beech wood blades. Thirty to forty-five minutes of hand cranking produced the ice cream. The adults could keep relays of us children cranking with promises of the reward for our efforts, which was the ice cream. When I try to call back some memory of the taste of that ice cream, however, I come up blank.

I distinctly remember details of the time and setting, the summer sundown with fireflies flashing their arcane communiqués to their own as we gathered under the weeping willow tree, but the taste has slipped away like a surreptitious nighttime visitor.

Once – and only once – my mother added fresh sliced peaches to the ingredients to create peach ice cream. We all complained about the taste. My brothers and I were growing up with appetites as provincial as our father's. We didn't know that five-dollar pints of Ben and Jerry's outrageous ice cream flavors lay in our future. So in the fifties we invariably made vanilla ice cream over which we poured Hershey's chocolate syrup. It seems like we could have made chocolate ice cream with the Hershey's added to the initial ingredients, but I can't remember that we ever did. Dad must have preferred vanilla. He was a vanilla kind of man, and his taste buds determined what all the rest of us ate. Now as an adult, I have encountered middle age and older people who believe an espresso beverage with Hershey's chocolate syrup poured into it is a mocha latte. Their cuisine lexicon must be governed by happy childhood memories of Hershey's viscous syrup stirred into milk or poured over ice cream.

15

What Was Really on Our Dinner Table

WE NEVER ATE in restaurants; we had no money for that. My parents rationalized that it was cheaper for our family, then totaling six, to grow or otherwise gather much of our own food and cook it ourselves. My mother usually prepared everything we ate. This sounds healthier than living it was.

I don't think I ever saw Mom use a recipe. Despite that, my former sister-in-law unearthed and turned over to me an old wooden box of what she thought were my mother's and Mammoo's recipes. The contents of the box proved to be hand-written index cards and scraps of paper with what I would consider to be food preparation suggestions rather than recipes. Quite a few call for combinations of ground meat and cans of Campbell's soup. I don't recall there being any other brand of soup available. Many instruct the preparer to "cook," no method specified or "bake," no temperature or length of time identified. They have names like shipwreck and doggy dinner, both of which I remember being served as a child. My husband thought they looked like Depression era recipes. Very likely they

135

are. That's when my grandmother and mother were initially cooking and serving these dishes.

It was during our tenure in Marshall that I became aware by increments that my family was considered to be poor. I think our meals reflected that. Shipwreck and doggy dinner still appeared on our table during the supposed prosperity of the post WWII fifties. Shipwreck was a mélange of ground meat, potatoes, green beans (or any available vegetable) and a can of Campbell's tomato soup baked together in the style of a casserole. Doggy dinner was fried ground meat and white gravy mixed together and poured over mashed potatoes or toast.

Chicken and pork chops were relatively cheap then and plentiful. Needless to say, we ate plenty of both – always fried, of course. At one point when we were raising our hogs, I can recall the market price of pork falling to eleven cents a pound. With that kind of return on my parents' investment, it cost us more to shelter and feed our pigs than we could recoup by sending them to market. Still, we didn't slaughter them for our own table. At Thanksgiving and Christmas dinners, we joked about serving roast-suckling pig with an apple in its mouth – next year. It remained a jest, never acted upon. The store-bought turkey made its usual appearance on the succeeding Thanksgiving just as the store-bought ham returned the next Christmas. And, as usual, the women spent all morning cooking them, and the man of the house who was seated at the head of the table carved them by hand.

Another long-running family joke was that my mother could cut a pound cake into such thin slices that you could serve it at a large wedding reception, and the guests would be able to read Marshall's daily newspaper through each sliver of it. I imagine that it must have been discouraging for my mother to see one cake or pie, whose preparation ate up so much of her time, wholly consumed in one meal because it had to be divided among so many of us.

Mom's desserts were real, made from scratch, even the icing on the cakes. Boxed cake mixes were available by the fifties, but my mother didn't use them. I don't remember ever seeing cans of cake and cupcake frostings or icings or ready-made pie shells at the grocery store at that time. Those too were homemade of basic ingredients from the pantry or nearest farm stand. We whipped up frosting from powdered sugar, a little milk, and a splash of vanilla extract. For greater variety beyond white vanilla, food dyes and flavorings could be added. Once assembled, pie dough was rolled out by hand, pressed into glass pie plates and its edges crimped. Pie fillings were also real – with lemon curd or apples or cherries which had to be washed, peeled, cored, pitted, sliced or otherwise prepared by my mother.

I can't remember my mother ever buying candy or snack food for us. For a brief time, though, my brothers and I chanced upon a source for candy bars. South of us on Second Street, one or two houses off Archer Avenue, was Hobe (Hobart) Eitel's family-owned corner store. Like all convenience or corner stores of its ilk, it stocked a wide range of everyday necessities with a limited selection of brands, sizes, or flavors. When money grew scarce, our family ran a tab at Hobe Eitel's store. Mr. Eitel was basically extending us unsecured credit. We were allowed to take groceries or other items as we needed them. Their prices were written down on an itemized running tally, which my mother would pay down as she was able. Eitel's did not issue a store charge card, accrue interest on our unpaid balance, or mail out statements. If Mr. Eitel ever grew concerned about the amount of our debt, he could easily pick up his phone and call my mother or ask her in person when he saw her on the street or in the store to try to make a payment.

My brothers and I began dropping into Hobe Eitel's store almost daily to pick up candy bars, telling the clerk to, "put it on our tab." Can you imagine any child today running through a Jewel-Osco supermarket or Whole Paycheck (Foods) and nonchalantly telling the cashier to put anything on a tab? But our candy habit was not one our family could afford. If all four of us, myself and all three of my brothers, put a five cent candy bar on the tab on one day, that was twenty cents. Multiply that by five days a week and the amount added to the tab exploded to one whole dollar each week. Today that sounds like a laughably minor amount, but in the mid-fifties and for us it was a worrisome expenditure for something we didn't need. My mother didn't try to explain to us that we didn't have sufficient income to indulge in daily candy bars. In our family, the amount of money we had, where it came from, and how it was spent were matters – like where babies came from – not spoken of in the presence of little pitchers with big ears. Such issues were too embarrassing to be discussed except in whispers behind closed doors. And rather than have Dad find out we had been doing this, which would have been my mother's fault somehow, Mom marched into Mr. Eitel's store and directed him and his assistants not to ever let her children put anything on our family's tab in the future.

Occasionally my mother's attempts to be parsimonious in planning meals backfired unforgettably. Once she added chicken gizzards and other internal organs to her homemade spaghetti sauce. It smelled and tasted like it sounds. Dad must have complained. Mom never served anything like that again. In any case, chicken entrails are best set aside to be divined by the seers. Mom also made lime Jell-O with lima beans – once. Maybe she saw a can of lima beans, a vegetable that we never grew in our garden, and a box of lime Jell-O sitting side by side on her kitchen shelf and was struck by an ingenious impulse to combine them. Dad probably didn't like that either. Lime Jell-O with lima beans never reappeared. But I concocted something equally bad and comparably received. I made cherry Jell-O with shredded carrots. That combination is just as inexplicable. However, unlike Mom, I added double the amount of water the recipe called for and it never jelled. My mother relented, and let me pour it down the drain. She didn't even gripe about the starving children in China. Dad, of course and as usual, unleashed a tirade about our wasting his hard-earned money and our not appreciating his efforts to provide for us.

Some foods from my mother's kitchen were always served together. I don't know why, and, at the time, it never occurred to me to question these combinations. Now, though, I'm perplexed about what might have motivated them. I don't believe my mother was preparing and serving food in the manner of her mother because meals I ate at my grandmother's didn't offer these same pairings. So my mother must have found food guides elsewhere. This was in the fifties, a time still innocent of the influences wielded by Martha Stewart and the celebrity chefs of our current era. I may have to lay the blame on Betty Crocker as my mother's inspiration. The first Betty Crocker cookbook appeared in the fifties. Even before that, however, Betty had her own radio broadcast and TV show. To me, a Betty Crocker effect remains an unknown but not unreasonable possibility because the time frame corresponds to my mother's manacled viands in Marshall.

My mother's requisite food pairs included crushed pineapple in lemon or lime Jell-O and fruit cocktail in red Jell-O. So here you can see why lima beans in lime Jell-O and shredded carrots in cherry Jell-O precipitated rebellion. Additionally, Jell-O was supposed to be served sporting a dollop of mayonnaise. The mayonnaise was splatted by the spoonful upon each parfait glass filled with the jewel-bright dessert when my mother distributed them at the dinner table. I was allowed to avoid the mayonnaise because my mother knew I didn't like it. The mayonnaise was not considered wasted because it had never reached my plate. And I did eat the Jell-O like the good little girl I was.

Pork chops, always fried of course, after all they were meat, were always accompanied by applesauce. One sliced hard-boiled egg was always fanned out atop the serving bowl of cooked spinach. I did ask why we had to serve it that way, but Mom could offer no explanation whatsoever, never mind a convincing one, for that particular ritual. I was an adult before I discovered that spinach leaves could be eaten uncooked and incorporated into salads. We never ate salads nor ever bought salad dressings. We did grow lettuce and radishes but ate them unmixed and undressed as an addition to a meal. The carrots we grew, being vegetables, were boiled to death before we ate them. Tuna noodle casserole was always topped with crumbled potato chips. This was the only time and place potato chips were seen in our house. We never bought potato chips to eat as snacks. Tuna noodle casserole also required a can of Campbell's soup, most commonly cream of celery or cream of mushroom. We bought Campbell's soups weekly because of their versatility and because they cost ten cents a can.

Gravy was mandatory. Dad must have been particularly fond of it. My mother made it automatically. On the plus side, it covered a multitude of culinary tragedies: over-cooked dried-out meat, stiff potatoes with insufficient milk and/or margarine; even disagreeable vegetables could be doctored with the ubiquitous semi-liquid. Too bad it didn't work on Jell-O.

Something else never seen on our home menus were soft drinks of any kind. If one of us children suffered an upset stomach, Mom might douse us with a small glass of ginger ale or Coca-Cola served at room temperature and stirred until the carbonation went flat. It was a rare treat for me to accompany my best friend Karen home after school and have her mother serve us a glass (small of course) of Coca-Cola or Pepsi-Cola diluted with ice cubes. Occasionally, I enjoyed a coke or root beer of the kind that used to be assembled at the soda fountain of Marshall's one drug store. Cola or root beer syrup was placed in the bottom of a glass, which was then filled with carbon dioxide dissolved in chilled water. These fountain drinks were always served with ice. An eight-ounce glass of this Coca-Cola cost ten cents but a root beer, which cost the same amount, was served in a slightly larger, perhaps ten-ounce glass, so I often ordered that instead. For an additional five cents, it was possible to order a vanilla, cherry, lemon, or marshmallow-flavored coke. If I had sufficient money to indulge in a marshmallow coke, I knew I should be prepared to quickly suck up the first few ounces. For some reason, the addition of the marshmallow flavoring set off a fizzy eruption of the drink over the edge of the glass. The soda jerk always set glasses of marshmallow cokes on a plate to catch the overflow.

My mother didn't have the time or patience to teach me how to cook. I left home at eighteen not knowing how to so much as fry an egg. My brothers and I were only in her way if we tried to participate in preparing dinner. Sometimes, though, Mom let my brothers and me help her make cookies. I gag now to think how we pleaded with her and bickered with each other over who should be allowed to scrape up and eat the uncooked dough sticking to the sides of the bowl and the beaters of her hand mixer. Back then, I don't recall anyone ever fretting about raw eggs harboring salmonella.

My siblings and my own contribution to the production of meals was to set and clear the table and wash and dry the dishes, by hand of course. When our grandparents acquired a dishwasher, we wanted to get one also. "We already have dishwashers," Dad told us. "They're named Judy, David, and Brad." I can't answer for my brothers, but I didn't appreciate the joke. There were at least the six of us sitting down for every supper every day of the week. Food was set on the table in serving bowls. So supper generated dirtied cooking pots and pans, serving bowls, plates and glasses, and serving and eating utensils. Being the immature, self-centered child that I was, I selfishly felt put upon when compelled to wash or dry all of that. I disregarded the fact that my mother had been doing both chores for every meal of every day of her married life until I was tall enough to reach into the sink. And that was in addition to her preparing from scratch every meal that we ate.

16

One Town – Many Strangers

I WAS A changeling. I had been certain of that. I rationalized that I must have been sent home from the hospital with the wrong family. Superficially I looked like my so-called parents, my own short stature, slim build, and dark hair and eyes a replica of theirs. But I felt like I existed in a Plexiglas cage that prevented me from connecting to this family to which fate had chained me. With the birth of each succeeding brother, I sensed my visibility as a distinct person evaporating. I suspected that I was increasingly perceived as a stock character. Because I was the oldest and a girl, I became little mother and resident baby sitter. I could never falter, disappoint an adult, display fear, or incite or express anger. I could behave as nothing other than a clean, respectful, diligent, dutiful prig of a little lady because I was a little version of a lady, and the decade of the fifties had such expectations of me. Besides, I always had to set a good example for my siblings.

It appeared to me that my brothers, particularly David, always received the best presents, the fried chicken drumstick, the largest slice of cake, the most attention, or the extra goodnight kiss. They were given "boy toys" like Lincoln Logs and BB guns that were inappropriate for me to play with. I was ordered to share my toys with the boys if they wished to play with them but called a selfish crybaby if I cried when one of them broke any of my playthings. Perhaps, like the Beatles' and Buddy Holly's renditions of "Crying, Wishing, Hoping" I thought that extending love begets love. I suggest it because I used to display great affection towards David. I know, and I knew well even then, that Mom liked David more than me. So I was wishing and hoping that exhibiting an attachment to David would gain me some of the overflow of devotion that poured from our mother upon David. I believe my mother loved me. She just didn't like me. When she was pregnant with me, she wanted a boy. But I wasn't. And then, I wasn't even a proper little girl. I wasn't a girly girl; I was a tomboy.

After school, my classmates reassembled at the candy store or gathered for study dates in each other's homes or at the library. Meanwhile, I sped home to entertain, feed, and change the diapers of whichever brother was the current baby. My parents required me to wash dishes, clean house, hang laundry, and iron my own as well as everyone else's clothes. My mother claimed that I ironed the boys' shirts better than she did. My brothers, on the other hand, were excused from such girl's chores while having no compensating boy's chores.

All my young life I asked myself why my mother didn't like me and why my parents blatantly favored my brothers. They were embroiled in as many, if not more, childish escapades than I ever was. Still, less was expected of them and fewer restrictions were placed on them. I constantly compared myself with David. I was as smart as David. I got straight As in school too. I was politer and more obedient than David. My pervasive sense of alienation became stained with resentment. I was obsessed with the perceived unfairness of my situation. Had I been able to see past my own self-absorbed misery as a child and adolescent, perhaps I could have discerned then what is now transparent. I was an outlier within a jumble of my similars. Why is perception so much clearer in one's rear view mirror?

There was Frank, for example. His last name remains unknown to me now as it was then. In fact, I can't even recall what he looked like. He was an age-mate of Pappy's and had resided in Marshall since they were children. Frank lived in a shanty without indoor plumbing at the north end of Second Street, which made him our close neighbor. Occasionally my father and my great-uncle Lauf paid him to perform day labor at what we called the poultry house. The poultry house, located across the street from the Courthouse Square and a block from the City Band Stand, was the combination workplace and warehouse of Dad and Uncle Lauf's wholesale poultry and egg business. It was where they kept their egg-grading machine and other equipment and accumulated the pullets and eggs for delivery to the big city resellers.

Frank always ate his dinner at one of Marshall's two restaurants, usually the greasy spoon diner rather than the more upscale Tom's Family Restaurant. This meal involved a certain ritual. Frank would earnestly peruse the bill of fare, pretending not to be the illiterate that he was.

For their part the waitresses, who included my mother when our strained finances compelled her into the work force, pretended to offer suggestions regarding the menu selections. "Our special for today is meatloaf with mashed potatoes and gravy. Or the breaded pork chop with applesauce is good tonight. And be sure to save room for the apple pie a-la-mode we have for dessert."

If Frank "read" the menu upside down, the servers heeded that not. Frank solemnly chose and ate his food, and – with deft assistance from the cashier – paid his bill and departed the restaurant with his dignity undamaged.

Unlike the Forsythes and most of Marshall's other citizens, Frank appeared to have no relatives. I'm not aware, though, that his apparent lack of family ever prompted anyone to invite him over to share their holidays or participate in their weekend card parties or even to sit with them of an evening on their front porch. I wonder now, did he regard himself as not belonging to the warp and weft of Marshall's citizenry? Did he feel sorry for himself? If I wrote him into a fictional novel, I could conjure forth a story as would supply answers to any questions his circumstances generated.

Suspicious others included our neighbors James Jones, Lowney Handy and the Handy Writers' Colony. The colony buildings were erected on a cow pasture owned by the mother of Harry Handy, Lowney's husband. Mr. Handy's mother owned a house on Archer Avenue. A precipitous gully separated her backyard from the unused cow pasture. The writers' barracks at the colony and Jim's house when he built it in 1953 would have been sited on North First Street if that street didn't peter out just after crossing Archer Avenue.

One summer day, David and I ambled into a stand of saplings behind one of the colony barracks. There we chanced upon a track laid down by apparently regular comings and goings through the underbrush. "That's the path from Lowney's cabin to Jim's," David informed me. Perhaps those weren't his exact words because they seem innocuous on the surface. But whatever words he spoke, or the manner in which he expressed them, or the knowing smirk on his face revealed to me that he was aware Lowney and Jim's relationship was more than that of promising writer and worldly mentor. His insinuation was that they had a sexual relationship.

"That's impossible," I contradicted him. To my naïve mind that didn't sound credible. Lowney was almost two decades, seventeen years to be exact, older than Jim. Besides which, Lowney was married to Harry Handy. In addition, I was beyond naïve at that time because I believed there existed some barrier that prevented males and females from engaging in sexual interactions with anyone other than their legal marriage partner. All that I've read about Lowney and Jim since then, however, concretely establishes that they carried on a fifteen-year affair and everybody – except me I guess – knew the nature of their interconnection. Even Harry Handy knew. Harry and Lowney had an open marriage long before I could comprehend what that entailed.

I recognized and could observe Jim and Lowney as they went about their public business. Otherwise, I knew little about them except the innuendo that drifted through adults' overheard conversations, like the odious miasma emanating from Velsicol. Lowney was a rangy woman with dark blonde hair and lively dark eyes in an angular face. The many available pictures of Jim depict him exactly as I remember him. With his broad shoulders and square face, close cropped dark blonde hair and deep-set eyes, he reminds me of an English bulldog. The single word that I think best describes the impression Jim and Lowney made upon me both then and now is intense. They always appeared to exist in a state of non-dual consciousness, fully engrossed in their present moment.

I was aware that Frank was atypical, the Handys and Jim distinctively unconventional, and I a changeling. But I failed to appreciate the stranger closest to me, the outlander fixed firmly and deeply in my life. That was my mother. She had been born, but more importantly raised, in Chicago. For her, living in Marshall must have been like being held hostage in a foreign country. For her, Marshall was a small town filled with prying eyes. Unlike Chicago, no one lived anonymously in Marshall. Even persons unknown to my mother knew her name and where to find her. The in-laws were intrusive. The farm animals were scary. The local yokel's notion of a social gathering was the Elks and Moose Lodge dinners of Easter Bunny laced with buckshot. They told Mommy it was chicken. Then they laughed at her when she cracked her tooth enamel on buckshot pellets and spit the offending mouthful back onto her plate. She may have been a Chicago girl, but even she knew you didn't kill chickens with a shotgun.

If only. How many times can I say that but still never be able to damn the river of time and redirect its current through another channel? If only I had been less self-centered and more self-aware. If only I could, with my current more mature discernment, fall back through time to revisit those persons, especially my mother. If only my mother were available to hear me say, "I didn't understand your role in my life until death removed you. I didn't recognize that you were the dynamic fire on the hearth and that yours was the radiating energy that animated us all." I didn't understand then and missed every opportunity thereafter until all that can be said now is, "Too late, much too late." My best hope may be that, as some faiths believe, we do indeed reconnect in some sort of subsequent world, one in which we make amends for our failings in our previous flawed incarnations.

17

Last Retreat

I DON'T RECALL a time in Marshall when Jim, Harry and Lowney Handy, and the Handy Writers' Colony weren't present in my backyard. Like a long driveway, a single lane gravel road branching off Second Street between the homes of Adie Thornburgh and Aunt Bertha Kannemacher provided vehicular access to the colony. Our mostly uncultivated land, the colony's grounds, and Jim's manicured two-acre lawn shared an undifferentiated common boundary with no fences, signs, or any other indicators marking where our property ended and theirs began. These conjoined lands formed a forty-five degree angle abutting the north and west edges of the Thornburgh, Kannemacher, and McNary properties. A white wooden fence separated those neighbors' backyards from the property upon which Jim later situated his high-priced bachelor pad.

Jim became Marshall's richest and most famous citizen with the publication of his novel *From Here to Eternity* in 1951. I was certainly aware that *Eternity*, Jim's first published book, was an overnight success. But only as an adult did I learn that it was the sudden and enormous popularity of Jim's novel that emboldened Lowney and Mr. Handy to establish Lowney's dream of a summer camp for writers. There Lowney could deploy her apparently winning methods to develop other authors. Jim invested sweat equity and royalties from his book in their venture.

The colony began as a wood barracks with Spartan individual rooms, very like monks' cells, for the writers. With the passage of time, a second barracks, dining ramada, and swimming hole were added. The swimming hole was basically no more than that: a hole bulldozed into the ground, its sloping sides plastered with concrete. Dirt and debris washing over its edge from snow melt and rainstorms transformed the colony's swimming hole into an oversized mud bath. The pool's overflow emptied into the same stream as the overflow from the lake on our property.

At precisely noon every day, we heard the single peal of a bell announcing the writers' lunch hour. Otherwise, the writers in residence there were quiet, unobtrusive neighbors. Apart from Jim, I don't believe I ever met any of the men – Lowney accepted only men into her program – who submitted themselves to Lowney's tutelage. Years later, I read that Lowney permitted her group of aspiring authors to leave the colony grounds once a week to walk into Marshall's uptown. Only Jim was excused from this as well as all other dictates from Lowney. Naïf that I was, I could still appreciate even then the rationale of situating a summer writers' colony on a cow pasture in a farm town with fewer than 3,000 residents. Distractions were few because Marshall had nothing to offer the hedonist. Its amenities consisted of two restaurants and the bars, and the community swimming pool when that was built. Cultural attractions were limited to the one-room town library and the lone movie theater until that burned down in 1957, the year I turned thirteen. To writers serious about their craft these seeming deficiencies were probably inconsequential. Presumably they brought with them the entertainments of their own created universes and dramatis personae.

In late 1950, while his book was undergoing final revisions at Scribner's, Jim had parked the trailer he was living in on the farmland in Marshall owned by Mr. Handy's mother. In 1953, Jim constructed his own home just outside the colony's grounds and alongside the gravel access road. The exterior of his modestly-sized house was a bricolage of stone, glass blocks, white clapboard, and maroon shingles. Jim invited my father inside for a tour. Dad reported to us that Jim's house had only four rooms, two downstairs and two upstairs. I think it was also about that time that Jim affixed a small white sign reading "Last Retreat" over the gateway of the colony's white wooden fence.

Jim was unable to attend college because his family suffered serious financial losses during the depression. Believing he had no better option, Jim enlisted in the peacetime army, but he chose to reside in Marshall upon his discharge from the armed services. I believe that Jim needed to be in Marshall coached by Lowney to write *From Here to Eternity*, although I can't provide a rational argument or empirical evidence to support that supposition. While living in Marshall, Jim also wrote and published his second novel *Some Came Running*.

My brothers and I were never allowed to read Jim's books, which my mother characterized as "meant for adults, certainly not for children." I clearly remember how the adults around me searched Jim's written works for replications of conversations they might have had with him (and yes they believed they found some), and for fictional characters based on someone they might recognize. A writing coach of my acquaintance called Jim's oeuvre iconic. I consider the widespread popularity of Jim's novels amongst my parents and grandparents' generations wholly explicable. He wrote in accessible language about the kind of people and places with which they were familiar. He wrote about experiences they had participated in. Jim was an author of the working class who wrote about people in conflict, specifically the total immersion hostilities of World War II.

Jim didn't spend all his days writing in solitude. He was unpretentious, approachable, and seemed to like to quiz ordinary people about their work and their lives. He joined the rest of us at the stores and in the bars, at the swimming pool, and in our homes. Once Jim invited himself to my ballet class where he sat quietly in a corner observing our lessons. Not even our mothers ever came to watch their awkward ducklings who each aspired to be the principal ballerina of the Bolshoi Ballet's *Swan Lake*. Any such activity on Jim's part launched rabid speculation that whatever he was then writing must be about that particular activity.

I didn't know until years later so much as one other writer who spent time at the Handy Writers' Colony, but we all knew Jim. He attracted everyone's attention and not merely because he was famous and wealthy. He, and Lowney as well, seemed both ordinary and exotic. Ordinary because they were both born in Robinson, Illinois, whose small town environment was similar to Marshall's and because of the everyday activities we saw them engaged in. But they were extraordinary in their personal relationship and in the import accorded to their actions by everyone around them. Typical of small towns, my family knew almost everybody living there just as they knew us. This commonality prompted us to notice and discuss each other, but only episodically. Most of us had to engage in some aberrant behavior to attract the constant scrutiny Jim and Lowney were subject to. If my brothers were seen sneaking a cigarette behind the garage, the observer called my mother. When David tried to start a campfire in the backyard and set the whole field of summer-parched grass ablaze, neighbors called the fire department.

Jim and Lowney, on the other hand, were cynosures, watched and talked about by everyone at all times. If I jumped off the diving board at the swimming pool, it was an unremarkable event unless I slithered out of my bathing suit while doing it. When Jim approached the diving board in his skimpy red Speedo, we all paused to observe his prowess. He was an excellent diver. He stopped by our house one afternoon wearing that same bright, little Speedo and sandals and nothing else. It took Mammoo, who chanced to be visiting us that week, twenty-four hours to recover. She was modest in the extreme and Jim, let me just say, sometimes liked to play the provocateur.

Additionally, Jim's work product was incomparable to that of anyone else we knew. When we consumed Gramma's tomatoes, Mrs. McNary's sweet corn, or drumsticks from Mom and Dad's chickens, that tomato, ear of corn, or drumstick ceased to exist. As we picked our teeth afterwards, we had no more to say than how favorably it did or did not compare to others of our experience. Likewise our menfolk. Unless they were farmers or engaged in farm-related enterprises, we generally had no idea what they produced during their eight-hour day outside the home. Jim's creative output, his novels, however, were dispersed beyond his local community into the literate universe to be consumed, and not just seasonally, but for generations into the future. As recently as October 2013, Tim Rice produced and wrote the lyrics for a musical based on Jim's book – not the movie – *From Here to Eternity,* which previewed at Shaftesbury Theatre in London. I feel that Jim would have been pleased. He was unhappy with the movie depiction, which he believed diluted important themes, homosexuality for one, which he had explored in his book. The book itself had already been sanitized for publication.

After my mother pored over *From Here to Eternity* and Jim's successive books, she passed them on to family and neighbors – adults only, of course. Along with the weather or the market price for pork, I now overheard them discuss the dialogue, characters, structure, and story arc of a literary work. And they speculated how Jim might incorporate their last conversation with him into his next novel, or that he had run out of ideas to mine from World War II and now was writing about ballerinas, for instance.

I can't overlook Lowney. At the time I didn't understand every facet of her ties to Jim, but I sensed that each amplified the attention paid to the other. Nonetheless, even apart from her connection to Jim, she was a remarkable woman. Unlike my mother and most women I saw around me, Lowney did not in any way conform to the fifties ideal of womanhood. She was one of about three women in Marshall that I knew personally who was not a mother and housewife. She had an identity independent of any man, child, or kitchen. She strode around Marshall trailed by whispers and vigilant eyes, and in a mist of disapproving but keen curiosity. Knowing Lowney and Jim in the repressive fifties suggested to me that it might be possible to follow a different path. Perhaps I didn't have to live my mother's life. I may not have been able to articulate it then, but Lowney and Jim demonstrated that you didn't have to let the era's conventions determine your choices in life. It was possible to transform the fate into which you had been born, and to diverge from the pattern your gender and your epoch prescribed.

❦

In approximately 1957 or 1958, compelled by financial necessity, my father sold most of the fourteen acres behind our house, including the barn, corn-crib, pig lots, and the lake to Jim. Neither Jim nor the Handys extended their white wood fence across what used to be our back lot. The barbed wire fence that enclosed the big pig lot remained untouched. Mom and Dad warned my siblings and me on several occasions not to cross that line, whether invisible or physically marked, since the land and buildings that used to be our playground no longer were. Jim himself never seemed to notice whether we played in what was now "his" barn or stripped the berries from "his" elderberry bushes in "his" pig lot.

Jim's "Last Retreat" proved not to be. In February 1957 he married Gloria, an Italian woman, whose last name was deemed by I don't know who to be so long, foreign, and saturated with vowels as to be unpronounceable by such as lived in an Illinois farm town. They surrendered to their presumed ignorance and called her by the nickname Moss, a corrupt, foreshortened version of her patronymic Mosolino. Gramma, to whom Jim introduced Gloria at the drugstore, as well as all the adults around me, agreed that she was attractive and vivacious. Jim and Gloria departed Marshall abruptly in mid 1957, eventually relocating to Paris, France.

My family moved from Marshall back to Chicago at the end of 1958. There, our numbers having increased to seven with the birth of Timothy, we found ourselves shoehorned into the Sineni family's basement, and residing with our new landlord's furnace, laundry tubs, and wine press. There was no girly pink bedroom for my mother's only little girl. Instead there were two bedrooms, one for my parents and one for the children, plus a living room and a kitchen. In our new home in someone else's basement, there was no place for any of us to escape from each other's company. And, unfortunately, we didn't like each other well enough to want to spend any more time together than we had to. What I missed most, though, was the spaciousness of the land and the benign neglect I had enjoyed there because of my parents' inability to see for the entire twenty-four hours of any one day within that expansive landscape where I was or what I was doing and with whom. And I quite simply missed the primitive pleasure of seeing, smelling, hearing, and being embedded in Marshall's physical actuality.

18

What I Did on My Summer Vacation – I

WHAT I DID on my summer vacation was the predictable topic for a speech or written essay every August in Marshall when we returned to school classes from those selfsame vacations. My summers included one inevitable ritual: vacation bible school. Ours could not be described as a religious home. My parents made no claims of adherence to any faith. My immediate family never attended church services, not even on Ash Wednesday, Easter, or Christmas. No devotional pictures, statues, or shrines graced our walls, shelves, or nightstands. Our yard, which covered several acres, boasted no Virgin Mary or St. Francis sculptures. We did not say grace before meals. Nor did my brothers and I recite that pre-scribed children's bedtime prayer: "Now I lay me down to sleep; / I pray thee, Lord, my soul to keep. / If I should die before I wake, / I pray thee, Lord, my soul to take." Nonetheless, every summer found me tramping off to vacation bible school.

Before moving to Marshall, we lived for one year in Indianapolis. During that year my mother went to Catholic mass sporadically. My brothers and I promised improbably proper behavior if she would take us with her. I was in first grade that year, so I was most likely six, David was four, and Brad two or three. Rather than even attempting to oversee a trio of such young children in a sacred space, Mom usually left us at home in Dad's care. We were so afraid of him that the three of us clustered in the corner of our fenced-in backyard furthest from the house and closest to the back gate for the duration of her absence. We didn't depart from our huddle in that corner until we caught sight of Mommy when she once again turned into our alleyway in, as we would name it in Marshall, her 'Sunday-go-to-meet'n' dress and straw bonnet with the thin, black, velvet ribbon and faux fruits circling its brim.

I can remember accompanying her to mass once or twice. Those few pilgrimages amazed the ingenuous child that I was then. Attendance at the Catholic mass of that era was, for me, a perplexing undertaking, akin to penetrating the clandestine congress of a secret society. Scented vapors swirled around me. Massed banks of candles flickered in gloomy alcoves. All around me indecipherable choruses of incantations and murmurs issued from the worshippers, my mother included, as they stood, sat, or kneeled to no logical pattern or purpose that I could discern. A man in a floor-length, black dress marched to the far end of the church past a short wooden fence where he mounted a dais. With his back to us, he furtively muttered and gestured before a linen-draped table, much as our own table would have been dressed for a holiday dinner. Heedful of my promise not to disturb her or other congregants, I dared not ask my mother for explanations. Besides which, being mystified provided more leeway for creative explications to bubble up in my imagination.

When we moved from Indianapolis to Marshall in 1951, there to reside amidst Dad's army of relatives, my mother gave up church attendance altogether. Instead she sent emissaries. Mommy did that sort of thing. For instance, she would schedule dental appointments for herself. She had, however, a significant fear of dentists. So, on the day of her appointment, she would look around and cry out, "Judy" or "David, go to the dentist!" The dentist was initially perplexed when, rather than our mother, David or I appeared for her appointments. But we, and he, adjusted, especially since he could charge for whoever occupied his dental chair. But this arrangement ended when Dad was handed a two hundred dollar dental bill. I had inherited my father's rotten teeth gene, and the dentist was finding cavities upon my every visit. Dad ordered Mom not to send me to the dentist again – and she didn't. I had no further dental care for ten years, by which time I was self-supporting and could ante up my own money to salvage my remaining teeth.

Likewise, but for different reasons, she sent my brothers and me for religious indoctrination instead of going herself. By doing so, she sidestepped losing a chunk of time in her busy enough days. Also her behavior still placed herself within the parameters of the good mother who tended to the religious edification of her children. It was in Marshall that my mother first endeavored to enroll David, Brad, and me in Saturday CCD classes. CCD (Confraternity of Christian Doctrine) is the religious teaching program of the Catholic Church, normally intended for school age children attending secular schools. The nuns almost immediately rescinded our registration because we were "rowdy and set a bad example for the other children," docile cradle Catholics all. My brothers and I weren't aggrieved by this unfortunate turn of events. We hadn't been thrilled to find ourselves in what seemed to us like one more elementary school class and on a Saturday at that.

But this business didn't end because the nuns rejected us. All the churches in Marshall offered free, one to two week, open enrollment vacation bible school programs during the summer. After our disgraced ejection from CCD classes, our mother began signing us up for vacation bible school with, dare I say, religious fervor. Mommy was wholly unbiased when it came to matching her children up with these spiritual offerings. If the Methodist church offered a program in May and the Congregationalists did so in June and the Millenarians and Holy Rollers had theirs in July, she registered us for all of them in succession. Did the parishioners cast themselves down upon the threadbare carpet of the chancel and froth at the mouth while shrieking gibberish? Did the congregation dance around the altar with snakes clenched in their teeth? Who cares? Mommy certainly didn't. Dogmas and rituals were irrelevant. All she wanted to know were the dates and times of their programs.

Just as keeping both my own and my mother's dental appointments failed to improve my teeth, my summers in vacation bible school were unsuccessful in leaving any discernable imprint on my spirituality. Or even on my memory. I can't recall what activities I engaged in or the lessons I learned there. I didn't mop spittle from the church's holey floor coverings or socialize snakes. I'm certain I would have remembered that much. I do have vague recollections of listening to bible stories and weak attempts at memorizing appropriate bible verses, the Lord's Prayer, the books of the Old and New Testament, as well as Psalm 23, the Lord is my shepherd. But, perhaps, I misremember, and such rote learning was undertaken in

Sunday school to which my mother also dispatched me. It seems like a good guess that indoctrinatory pursuits would have been similar in both venues.

One thing I did note both then in Marshall's vacation bible schools and in the cities and suburbs wherever I attended religious services or bible study groups as a young adult: each and every one of these churches claimed that it was the one true church. I encountered that identical assertion in every denomination – that it was the authentic descendent of the Christian community founded by Jesus and his disciples. All other claimants to that appellation were declared to be fraudulent or misguided, and those sorry flocks of believers were missing the boat of salvation. In light of that, I could imagine that the dearly-held truisms of all these good Christians as well as those of all others persons, my own included, are regarded by someone somewhere as meritorious of incarceration, a straight jacket, or burning at the stake. These multiple conflicting attestations provoked my distrust of religious institutions. If the message of any one of these sects wasn't sufficiently cogent to compel the fealty of all persons throughout the world, why should I be convinced either?

But after spending a second summer in Marshall's vacation bible schools, a certain one of my evolving suspicions began to solidify. My parents had never displayed one iota of interest in any church denominations or in spirituality in general. If prodded by clergy, my mother agreed that the religious instruction of one's children was desirable, but, otherwise, neither Mom nor Dad ever spontaneously expressed the necessity of faith-based indoctrination for my brothers or me. That being the case, I started to wonder if Mommy's unstated purpose for sending us to these summertime church programs was to remove us from her life for at least a few hours each summer weekday. I don't feel sad for myself or angry with her if that was her intent.

Now as an adult myself, I can appreciate my mother's circumstances. Living in a dilapidated, ten-room house with an expanding brood of toddlers and elementary school age children but with no household help whatsoever and none of her own family within two hundred miles, every unmade bed and unwashed dish was probably perceived by my mother as one more burden; each whiny baby and frown from her in-laws one more confirmation of her inadequacy. The school in vacation bible school was then as now an excellent justifier for any pursuit. The bible in vacation bible school was the oriflamme, the principle or ideal, of the good mother's *izzat* or reputation. The vacation in vacation bible school was Mommy's – from the encumbrances of the title of "Mother" that she had shouldered as a twenty year old and had borne as she staggered through the rest of her foreshortened life.

One thing that I did learn from her, and that I still have implacable faith in, is that my mother had a wicked sense of humor.

19

What I Did on My Summer Vacation – II

THERE WAS MORE to summer vacation than vacation bible school. Marshall's public library, which occupied one large second floor room of a storefront building on Archer Avenue, provided a summer reading program of sorts. No recommended or suggested reading list was provided. We could choose to read any book we desired or that met our mother's approval. Each child was given a single page cartoon of a segmented "bookworm" wearing eye-glasses. We printed our name on these sheets that the librarian then affixed to the ends of bookcases. For each book we read, we received something like a green star to lick and stick to fill out our bookworm, segment by segment. There were no prizes other than flaunting our sticker-filled bookworm. I charged through as many of the Nancy Drew and Judy Bolton girl-detective series, and galloped through all the Marguerite Henry's horse tales as I could find. I was fond of historical novels, so I read whatever of Sigrid Undset and Alexandre Dumas *père* was available in the library. Then, intent on reading my way around the bookcase-filled room, I started with *Anthony Adverse* by Hervey Allen which was lodged on the first shelf. I remember making it through *Raintree County* by Ross Lockridge Jr. Reading just that book – all 1,060 pages of the original edition – demonstrates the depth of my immersion even as a pre-teen in the worlds to be found between the covers of books.

Being in farm country meant that Marshall's school year was calibrated to the area's growing season. We began school in August and finished the school term in May. Our environment determined most of our summer activities. When not reading or in church, I spent my summer vacations outdoors with the land, the elements, the flora and fauna. My family raised pigs and chickens. At various times we also possessed a white-faced Hereford heifer, a goat, a rabbit, and a mole. And, like most people in Marshall, we had a dog. People in Chicago thought we must have lived out in the country on a farm. We didn't. Our property was considered to be in town, but we occupied fourteen acres of mostly uncultivated land with no houses or streets behind us.

My mother had been born and raised in Chicago. Of all Marshall's small town traits, the one that may have irked her most was everyone's interconnectedness. No one of us lived there anonymously as we may do in the larger realm of Chicago. Everyone knew not only who we were but also what animals we owned and where to find us. So the phone calls from all those human watchdogs annoyed my mother when they called to report things like, "Mrs. Forsythe, your heifer is in my garden" or "Elaine, your goat is on my front porch." And their point was that she should do something about the situation.

Once, though, my mother told them what to do. A neighbor a few blocks from us phoned to advise us that my blue-tick pointer puppy which neighbors at the end of Second Street had given me just a few months previously was in their yard and seemed to be ill. "Call the police and tell them to shoot her," Mom replied and hung up on them. When she saw tears welling up in my eyes, my mother turned on me like a Mafioso enforcer. She shook her index finger in my face sternly ordering me, "Don't you cry. Don't you dare cry." I fled to the bathroom to wipe any evidence of tears off my face and to blow my nose. Five minutes later, I returned to the kitchen to continue whatever we had been doing before that phone call. Neither of us mentioned the puppy. Mom and I both understood that the police would dump the dog's body atop the haphazard heaps of Marshall's rubbish at the dump outside of town. After all, she wasn't a family member or income-generating livestock. She was only a dog, not something people living in a fifties farm town would get sentimental about.

⸺⸺⸺

The farm kids of Marshall tended to join the 4-H club. Like my siblings and myself, those of us who lived in town were more likely to become members of the Brownies and Girl Scouts or Cub Scouts and Boy Scouts. Some town kids did participate in 4-H, which encompassed gardening, cooking, and sewing in addition to breeding and showing farm animals common to our region, such as calves, swine, and sheep.

All that I can recollect of my tenure with the Brownies was the mandatory uniform, a brown A-line dress that buttoned down the front from collar to hem. Whatever activities I engaged in as a Brownie were eminently forgettable because that's what I have done with them. My brother David, on the other hand, learned practical things in the Cub Scouts and Boy Scouts, like how to start

165

campfires. At the zenith of one summer's heat and desiccation, he practiced kindling a campfire in the field behind our house. The native grasses, then commonly known to us as weeds, were seared from green to pallid yellow and lay prostrate upon the sunbaked earth. David neglected to clear away this mat of scorched vegetation. Instead, he laid a circle of tinder and larger twigs on top of it. He not only successfully started a campfire, but also managed to torch about an acre of our backyard. Neighbors and our hysterical mother hastily summoned the fire department. For Brad and me it was an exciting, but never repeated, event.

❦

Summer also brought out the guns. No one in our immediate family was a hunter. Others in the area did hunt rabbits, which explained why so many families owned beagle dogs. Some also hunted game birds and kept dogs like pointers and setters for that. It was also possible to shoot squirrels, opossums, raccoons, and pigeons. Pappy instructed my brothers and me, and we also learned by observation the practical aspects of how to safely carry, load, aim, and shoot rifles and pistols. Later, as a young adult, I also learned how to reload shotgun shells. I was aware of, but lacked the vocabulary then to articulate, some of the more technical details of firearms such as their power levels, effective range, and the attributes of their discharged pellets. Now, so much information from sellers of a more expansive range of weaponry than any seen in Marshall can be uncovered with a few keystrokes on a computer that one hardly needs to wade through any weapon's instruction manual.

One of the sons of my great-grandfather's second wife Edith – I believe it was Everett – passed through a phase of shooting our white Leghorn chickens off our hen yard fence with his .22 rifle. Chickens can't see in the dark so, when summer's dusk began to settle in, our hens went to roost. As a matter of course, we cut off the pinions of one of their wings and sometimes their longest tail feathers. Hindered by such lop-sided flying mechanisms, our hens were unable to fly far or high. As a result, some of our chickens roosted in the lowest branches (four feet from the ground) of the stunted tree in their enclosure and others on top of the five-foot tall wire fence encircling the hen yard. In the deepening gloom and with no intervening structures between our adjacent yards, our white Leghorns were easily visible and defenseless targets. In this case, it was my mother who grabbed the phone to let Edith know, "Your son is shooting at and killing our chickens roosting on our hen yard fence! Next time, it might be one of my young children shot and killed!" Having been raised by her, I can verify that my mother had an excitable temperament. I have no difficulty imagining how, in such a scenario, her voice would escalate to a high-pitched screech. The only component Edith would have been spared would be my mother's cigarette-yellowed index finger shaken under her nose. Everett's mischief ceased posthaste.

Guns were ubiquitous throughout the area and in every season, of course. Dad owned a multi-stroke pneumatic air pistol. It utilized compressed air as its energy source to propel metallic or plastic projectiles. An on-board lever pumped pressurized air into the pistol's reservoir. The model Dad possessed could achieve a variable power level for long or short range shooting with two to ten pumps of the lever. He tried shooting the pigeons off our house's tin roof; his best achievement was to draw blood on one of them. We could see a yard long ribbon of red ooze down a tin panel after the pigeon took flight. I remember pumping the gun's lever several times and firing it, perhaps with Dad's supervision but probably without. Once or twice, David and I snuck the pistol out of the house and hid in thickets of weeds far from the house to shoot the tallest plants with it, but not so many that Dad would notice the diminished number of pellets. Afterwards, we surreptitiously returned it to Dad's hiding place on top of the china hutch in the dining room. David's and my own urge to handle our father's gun arose from his withholding of it. If he had supervised our loading and firing it, I believe our curiosity would have been snuffed out. Instead, in accord with his disposition, Dad slapped his bullying "This is mine, and you can't make me share it because I'm bigger than you," sign on it. Our usual response was that whatever was too good to share with his own children must be worth the challenge of furtive exploration to uncover the qualities that made Dad's possessions exclusive to himself.

For boys, a BB gun was de rigueur, as much so as a doll might have been for a girl at that time. Therefore, at what my parents deemed an appropriate age, David, too, was given a BB gun. David lived in Marshall from ages four to ten. That demonstrates what was then and there considered an appropriate age. Most likely he received a Daisy Red Ryder. The Red Ryder, modeled after a western Winchester rifle, was sold in the United States as a toy. They generally had very low velocities of around 275-280 ft/s because of the weak springs used to keep the cocking efforts low for use by youths. Its effective range was about ten yards. David had to share his BB gun with Brad and, if he had dared to ask why, it was because

Mom and Dad said so, that's why. This also saved them from having to buy Brad, who was eighteen months younger than David, a BB gun of his own.

David and Brad might have tried shooting rabbits and squirrels, but the Red Ryder was a toy so they more commonly shot at inanimate non-moving targets which were easier to hit. One summer afternoon they decided to do just that. There should have been no drama to their decision. But apparently, they lacked a conventional bull's-eye target, or even a tin can with a bale of hay positioned behind it and set in the middle of the field behind the barn. A tin can on top of a fence post of the pig lots was verboten, glass bottles even more so. A BB pellet, rebounding can or flying glass shards might strike one of the sows or piglets. The pigs were one of Dad's income sources. Any unfortunate accident impacting them would subject its agent to Dad's most violent rage.

Forced to improvise, David's creative young mind – or the immature pre-frontal cortex of his brain – fastened upon Mom's oval, sixteen-inch diameter, and five-inch deep white enamel washtub. Brad held up this improvised target while David fired the first round. Steel BB pellets are prone to ricochet, especially off hard surfaces. Lead BB pellets bouncing off hard surfaces usually flatten and retain a large portion of their initial energy. A 0.177 standard lead pellet fired above 300 ft/s has skin-piercing capability. That potential increases with velocity but decreases with distance. It can leave a severe and painful bruise even without skin penetration. David's first shot hit the washtub, ricocheted, and grazed Brad's left cheekbone.

Brad was fortunate. The ricocheting BB barely pierced the thin skin over his cheekbone, but he suffered dramatic discoloration of his sub-ocular skin from the rupturing of underlying small blood vessels. Nothing, however, saved my brothers from the wrath of Mom. After she ascertained that Brad's eye had not been shot out, she fell upon both shooter and victim like one of the Furies of Grecian mythology. A whirlwind of slapping and swearing rained down upon them. She shook her finger in their faces and screamed, "Don't you ever do that again! You'll be sorry when your father gets home!" Even if Mom had neglected to mention it, Brad's bruise was impossible to camouflage and begged for explanation. I can't recall what did happen when Dad returned from work. I don't know if this infraction was sufficient to cost David his Daisy Red Ryder. As a youngster, Dad had deliberately shot his older brother with a BB gun, but I doubt that reminding him of that would have increased his empathy about this mishap.

Guns were so commonplace as to be as invisible as the air we breathed. To the best of my knowledge, there were no required gun licenses or background checks, and no shooting ranges. I don't recall anyone ever wearing protective eye goggles or hearing muffs. Somehow generations of us managed to survive into adulthood unscathed despite both Marshall's widespread gun ownership and the laissez-faire attitude towards them. Still and all, neither did any-one that I knew of possess assault rifles and multi-bullet magazines. No one carried their weaponry on their person at all times to intim-idate the rest of us or to settle disagreements. Nor did Marshall har-bor rival gangs, drug peddlers, disaffected minorities, or clusters of unemployed young males loitering on street corners, all of whom might feel the need for defensive hardware.

On a summer weekend we could pile into the car, or cars depending on how many relatives joined us, for an expedition out to Blizzard Ford to wash the vehicles. Three miles north of Marshall along Route 1, a bridge crossed Blizzard Creek. Blizzard Road, which was an automobile-width dirt track, forked away from Route 1 just past the bridge, and progressed west then northwest almost parallel to the creek. Fifty years ago, it was possible to drive down the embankment from Blizzard Road and out onto the gravel and sheets of sandstone that formed the creek bottom. Our flock of relatives could spend a hot, happy afternoon there. With some rags and soap, the adults had access to a free car wash. We youngsters might have helped, but we were more likely to enjoy ourselves wading in the creek, which flowed east under the bridge just fast enough to create a visible ripple. The water, ankle deep on me, lacked sufficient depth or rapidity to scare the adults into screaming at us that we would drown if we weren't careful. Besides which, they had each other's company to distract themselves. So we children waded back and forth near the bank of the ford gazing at the insects that skated over the water's surface and at the clusters of small fish below the water's surface that swerved away in unison to avoid us. In the soft gurgle of the passing current and drowsy drone of unseen insects, we observed the double-winged dragonflies and their dainty relatives the damselflies flitting about the littoral weeds. The sun was hot, the water was lukewarm, and everyone was relaxed and happy.

Blizzard Ford wasn't always so benign. One day, the creek overflowed due to severe storms in the area. Crossing the bridge spanning the creek was deemed unsafe for vehicular traffic. A crowd of us drove out to see for ourselves. We stood on the south end of the bridge and watched the engorged channel's now menacing brown water scouring slabs of earth from under the bridge's north footing as it rushed eastward well above its usual boundaries. The bridge seemed to shudder with each foot of the embankment that collapsed into the riding current. Or perhaps the sight and sound of the furious flood waters and subsidence of the riverbank made me shudder. I was seeing a portion of my familiar natural background turn sinister. But like a cheerful fifties sitcom, the bridge held and Blizzard Creek dwindled back down to its customary state of benevolence. Equilibrium was restored.

When I visited Blizzard Ford in 2011, much remained as I remembered it. The ankle-deep creek water flowing east under the bridge over the sheets of sandstone, even the dragonflies and damselflies waltzing around the forbs in the 90-degree heat abided. What I couldn't see was how we were ever able to drive down the embankment by the bridge. As I expected, there are more shrubs and saplings sprouting there now, but the slope of the riverbank looks too steep to allow a car to descend it safely. In pockets of dust on the sandstone shelf underlying the embankment and extending into the watercourse, I saw what appeared to be the faint tracks of an all-terrain vehicle. The area now looked like it would only be accessible to a vehicle such as that. But I know my imagination isn't overwhelming my memory about this. I have old photographs of four generations of my family gathered around some family member's 1940s automobile in the same shallow water of Blizzard Ford slightly west of the bridge that crosses northbound Route 1.

⚜

Occasionally, I trekked out past the Clark County Fairgrounds to the Dairy Queen on North Second Street. The Dairy Queen only offered soft-serve, what used to be called ice milk but which the Food and Drug Administration (FDA) now categorizes as reduced fat ice cream (five percent butterfat content). A small pineapple or strawberry sundae cost ten cents; my personal favorite, the burnt caramel sundae, cost fifteen cents. However, even that amount was more spending money than my brothers and I usually had access to, so those sundaes remained an infrequent treat for us. If and when I did have sufficient change, I could walk to the Dairy Queen on the sidewalk until it ended at the County Fairgrounds and then continue the remainder of the way along the side of the road, which wasn't heavily traveled.

Often though, my youngest brother Gordon and I used my bike to get there. A girl's bicycle, of course, because even bicycles were gender specific. Boy's bikes had a horizontal bar joining the front wheel frame and the seat; girl's bikes didn't. Gordon rode facing forward with his sit-down wedged into the basket of my blue, girl's bicycle and his feet propped on the part of the frame that covered the bike's front wheel as I peddled us down Second Street. Our irresponsible parents didn't ensure that we wore bicycle helmets. But at that time bicycle helmets were as foreign to us as Spanish and Polish, Chicago's unofficial second and third languages.

He and I were often seen doubled up on my bike that way, a fine example of the fair and the dark. His crew cut was as blonde as my ponytail was deep brown, and his eyes were the color of sky blue heaven instead of mud puddle brown like mine. His skin was also whiter than my own and readily tanned or burned by the sun. He was lanky and reached six feet by the time he was a sophomore in high school. At age thirteen, I grew one final inch to reach my adult height of five feet. From the time he learned to walk, Gordon tagged along just about everywhere I went in Marshall. Mom and Dad shunted him off onto me as much as possible, especially after Mom was forced by our straitened circumstances to become a waitress at one of Marshall's two restaurants. Gordon's constant company became as normal a part of my young life as my casting a shadow on a sunny day.

It makes me smile now to picture myself biking about town with that tow-headed boy, his long white limbs wrapped around my bike frame. He grew up to be such an easy-going laid-back adult that my husband described him as, "so laid-back he's nearly horizontal." Yet it was Gordon who stepped forward and took Pappoo in when the retirement home where my mother placed her father before she died called David to tell him, "we like Harry, but he just can't stay here any longer. He needs more supervision and services than we can provide." At that point my husband declared, "I took care of my father when he got old, so I know how much work that is. Gordon deserves to go straight to Heaven for doing this." Be that as it may, the passing years haven't been kind to Gordon. That cute blue-eyed tag-along who morphed into the to get along, go along adult is now confined to a prison half way across the country after pleading guilty to felonies too despicable for me to spell out.

⁂

When we moved to Marshall it had one movie theater. For a period of time, Mom allowed David, Brad, and me to attend the Saturday matinee. We happily sat through Looney Tunes cartoons and that week's feature film. Westerns and musical comedies were the predominant movie fare. We saw *Oklahoma*, *Singing in the Rain*, and films with Donald O'Connor and Francis the talking mule. I also remember seeing *The Seven Year Itch* with Marilyn Monroe, the nuances of which I'm sure I failed to comprehend, and *My Sister Eileen* (1955). The candy, popcorn, and sodas sold at the concession stand had not yet been labeled junk food or empty calories. It doesn't matter what it was called then because Mom never gave us extra change to buy any of it. Not only was there no money for such an unnecessary extravagance, but such snacks also rotted your teeth incurring further expenses for future dental work.

When the movie ended, we returned home to spend the remainder of the afternoon and the early evening watching the Saturday line up of westerns on TV. It was the era of western-themed movies, TV shows, toys, and other merchandise. Only two television channels were broadcast in Marshall, so we were fortunate to find two hours of programming we enjoyed. We watched *The Cisco Kid*, *Have Gun Will Travel*, *The Lone Ranger* and *The Roy Rogers Show*. While my brothers and I were burning our eyes out with hours of cartoons, the Saturday matinee and TV westerns, Mom and Dad retired to their bedroom to take an afternoon nap behind a closed door. They issued dire threats that the house better be burning down or blood gushing before we disturbed them. I was so naïve that I believed the part about the afternoon nap. I was sufficiently sophisticated, though, to take seriously their orders that we better not disturb them. I can't think of a single occasion that my brothers or I thought warranted doing so.

In 1957 when I turned thirteen the Saturday matinees ceased, for me at any rate. Children's admission to the matinee was twenty cents but at age thirteen the price rose to fifty cents. For a while my parents had been able to scrape together sixty cents for three of us to go to the movies every week. But fifty cents for me was more than they cared to pay. Sometimes in a surge of fairness, my mother would declare, "since Judy can't go to the show, the boys (David, Brad, and Gordon) can't go either." But in late 1957 or maybe it was in early1958, the movie theater burned down. It was never rebuilt, so, thereafter, none of us spent Saturday afternoon at the movies.

Infrequently, our whole family went to a drive-in movie. Admission was one flat price per car, no matter how many people were in it. Mom would dress us kids in our pajamas. If we felt embarrassed to be out of the house in our sleepwear, she assured us that nobody would look at a kid in pajamas, and we would be in the car and out of sight anyway. My parents' plan was that my brothers and I would fall asleep in the back seat, and she and Dad could sit in the front seat and watch the featured film. It must have worked because I can't remember any movies that we might have seen there. I do vaguely recall sitting on the hood or roof of the car through part of the evening, and the scratchy sounds emitted by the unwieldy metal speaker that we had to hang on one of the car windows, and the stack-up of honking cars all trying to exit the theater lot at the same time. Drive-in movies were an outing we seldom undertook. Perhaps, trying to confine three or four of us children in a car until it was sufficiently dark to project a picture on an outdoor screen required more patience than my father could muster.

❦

I'm not sure when it arrived, but a few years before we returned to Chicago, Marshall built an outdoor community swimming pool on North Second Street just outside the fairgrounds. My mother loved to swim, so she signed me up for swimming lessons every summer, the only season the pool was open. She sent me back yearly because I was so afraid of the water that I never learned to swim. Every time I put my face down on the pool water's rocking chlorinated surface, fear of my imminent suffocation by the treacherous heavy liquid overwhelmed me. My head and body would jerk away from the danger while my arms and legs flailed about seeking a solid surface. Mom seemed blind and deaf to my terror. She remained convinced that battering me with repeated swimming lessons would convert me from an aquaphobe into the little mermaid her daughter should be. Eventually I fell back on dog paddling, which didn't require putting my face in the water.

Every hour a pool attendant blew a whistle to signal all the swimmers to exit the water. For five to fifteen minutes, we had to rest at the edge of the pool in order to avoid swimmer's cramp that might lead to our death by drowning. There were adults only nights and one family night at the pool. Boys and girls had access to the pool on alternating afternoons. It was during one of those girls' days at the pool that I overheard the two school friends I came with discussing whether to stop at the snack bar. We were all in the changing rooms in separate stalls, so they couldn't see that I was near enough to overhear them. One classmate asked the other, "Should we skip the snack bar? Judy never has any money. If we buy anything, we'll have to share it with her, or we'll have to buy her something, too." I felt embarrassed to be reminded again that my family and I had noticeably less spending money than most people I knew. When the three of us met up at the exit, I didn't let on that I had heard their conversation. Instead, I told them that my mother wanted me to come straight home without detouring for treats that would spoil my appetite for supper.

For a week or two during the summer, usually alone or more rarely with David or Brad, I stayed with Mammoo and Pappoo in the three-flat apartment building they owned near 115th Street and Calumet Avenue in Chicago's Roseland neighborhood. Mammoo struggled to entertain me in their two-bedroom apartment and midget-sized back yard that lacked any outbuildings, animals, or environmental features. I helped Mammoo by overwatering her houseplants, and by refraining from putting my hands in the wringer of her Maytag wringer washing machine or under the hot water tap which gushed scalding hot water. In Marshall, we had to let the water run for ten minutes to achieve a lazy flow of lukewarm water.

If I left their yard, I was forbidden to step off the sidewalk. People in Chicago had lawns rather than yards and were irrationally protective of them. Nor was I allowed to walk any further than half a block in either direction from their building. Roaming as my brothers and I did in Marshall was categorically prohibited. Those were the years when "stranger danger" warnings were announced repeatedly; and in Chicago, unlike Marshall, most of the people around me were strangers.

Mammoo took me on the streetcar to Michigan Avenue to window shop. Being pulled through denser crowds than I had ever encountered, and of people twice as tall as me, was terrifying. Mammoo and I also strolled through a public park near the now retired Mendel High School for boys on 111th Street. I was not allowed to interact with any other children we might meet because of the widespread fear of contracting polio, for which a preventive vaccine did not yet exist. Pappoo mainly overlooked me but occasionally pulled his head out of his newspapers to make a comment about me to Mammoo.

One summer week when I was there with Brad, we badgered Mammoo into allocating each of us one-third of a wine glass full of the Dago red wine she kept in a wine carafe in her dining room hutch. Since it looked like Kool-Aid, we assumed it would taste like the cherry, strawberry, or raspberry Kool-Aid that Mom let us drink in summer. Our first sip, of course, proved that Mammoo was right when she warned us we wouldn't like it. Its alcoholic fumes choked us, and its alcoholic content torched our throats. Mammoo had to drink it for us, which she did in one slurp per glass. Brad and I were flabbergasted that she could do that without gagging.

When my family moved back into Chicago, David and I reversed the process by spending a few weeks of the summer with Gramma and Pappy in Marshall. Brad did not spend any of his summer vacation in Marshall because Gramma told Mom, "Don't send Brad. I don't want him to stay with us because he wets the bed."

Gramma adhered to the fifties stereotypical assignment of chores by gender. I was supposed to iron David's clothing, and he was supposed to polish my shoes. I possessed one pair of Buster Brown shoes and one pair of sandals. For one reason or another, David somehow never actually did polish my shoes. And evidently that was all right. I don't recall him ever being even mildly chastised for his non-compliance with Gramma's dictates. David, however, had more than two shirts and more than two pairs of slacks and/or shorts. It was not all right for me to not iron his clothes. Gramma ordered me around like a passive and obedient house servant who coincidently happened to be a relative. One of her orders was, of course, to iron David's clothes, which saved her from having to do so.

The most disturbing moments for me, however, were when Gramma directed me to iron Bomma's cotton housedresses but warned me not to tell Bomma. Bomma, in turn, would instruct me to call her when I finished pressing everything else, so she could iron her clothing. I was caught in the middle of their tug-of-war and endured recriminations no matter which one of them I obeyed. Perhaps, Gramma was trying to spare her aging mother from the heat and exertion involved in standing and sweeping a hot, heavy iron over damp, wrinkled dresses that had to be continually rotated on the ironing board and disentangled from the iron's electric cord. But it seemed less like kindness and more like controlling, especially when Gramma told me she wanted Bomma to stay in her bedroom.

At the end of summer, my brothers and I and all our age-mates returned to our classrooms when school resumed in August. The only signifier of summer's end and the immanent beginning of the new school term was the Clark County Fair held the last weekend of July. Except for that unofficial indicator, there were no back-to-school rallies attended by the Superintendent of Schools or city officials. There were no school open houses with free haircuts and eye exams. Nor were there handouts of backpacks filled with school provisions. In fact, none of us carried backpacks; we probably didn't know what they were either unless we saw them depicted in our brothers' Boy Scout manuals. Our parents weren't handed a three-page list of required school supplies. The news media wasn't filled with announcements of back-to-school sales and coupons for new school clothing and other necessities.

We were required to present proof that we were current on our childhood immunizations, far fewer in number at that time because there were none for measles, mumps, rubella (aka German measles) or chicken pox. My age-mates and I all acquired natural immunity to German and three-day measles, mumps, and chicken pox through having contracted those diseases. I believe that we were also required to undergo a physical exam for entrance into elementary and junior high school. These matters were readily attended to because we all lived in intact middle or working class families with access to Marshall's two general medicine practitioners. None of us were wards of the state, foster children, orphans, or living in a homeless shelter or under the viaduct. So, in August the school doors opened and we returned to our classes. It was that straightforward.

20

The Clark County Fair

THE CLARK COUNTY Fair held at the County Fairgrounds the last weekend of July and the first few days of August put the finish to our summer vacation and heralded the imminent onset of the school year. Marshall is the seat of and largest town in Clark County. The fair was a major event because it was the fair for the whole 505 square miles and fifteen townships that comprise Clark County. The fair offered horse racing, both harness and running under saddle; a western horse show with both horse and rider in western gear; livestock and home economics judging; tractor pulls; and a carnival. The carnival was a traveling amusement show presenting games of skill, which nobody had sufficient skill to win, a Ferris wheel, and cotton candy spun before an appreciative circle of salivating youngsters.

For me, the fair was a kaleidoscope of sensory tantalization. Best of all, my mother was willing and Dad actually wished to attend it, and they brought my brothers and me with them. My family usually walked around the fairgrounds before the fair officially opened. We watched the unloading and penning of the pigs, sheep, and calves in their barns, and peered into every occupied stall of the main and accessory horse stables. We moseyed through the temporary platforms in the cinderblock building where farmers' wives and daughters displayed their canned preserves, homemade peach pies, and hand-made quilts and embroidered doilies. We always returned for at least one evening as well as a weekend afternoon to watch the horse races and to discover who had won blue ribbons for their prize heifer or pickled watermelon rind.

David, Brad, and I were allowed to make one attempt each at no more than three game booths. We tried tossing the plastic ring resembling an embroidery hoop over an empty glass milk bottle, or pitching a nickel-size metal slug into a shallow clear glass saucer set on a drinking glass, or shooting a rifle at a rotating line of wooden ducks. It didn't matter how careful our aim or how much advice our parents poured over us, we missed more often than we scored. I never won the uberprize of a kewpie doll; neither did anyone else I knew. Once though, I was able to claim a folding paper fan by knocking down one of the ducks at the shooting gallery. From handling David's BB gun and Dad's air pistol at home, I knew to accommodate for the ever so slight deviation (maybe intentional) in the gun barrel, and to aim somewhat ahead of the moving line of birds so that my intended target collided with the rifle's discharged projectile. And, perhaps, that one evening that rifle discharged a viable pellet.

In contrast to the games of skill, the cotton candy never disappointed. I'm surprised that Mom agreed to buy it for us. She was usually quite vigilant about shielding us from anything that might result in a future trip to the dentist or doctor. Not that she was opposed to medical practitioners, just the money required to visit them. Perhaps Mom rationalized that cotton candy was, after all, mostly air and only appeared once a year with the fair. As a youngster, that was the only time and place I ever saw or tasted cotton candy.

All the children stood as close as possible to the cotton candy apparatus and its operator. While it was in operation, the machine emitted an alluring cooked sugar aroma that the finished product lacked. And at close range, we could behold the transformation of the granulated sugar and pink – it was always and only pink – food coloring into puffs of pink cotton. The molten sugar and food coloring were extruded through tiny holes in the central spinning head of the machine by centrifugal force. When it came in contact with the air, it solidified and built up on the inner wall of the surrounding bowl. The magician orchestrating the process twirled paper cones through the accumulating strands, gathering the pink cloud of spun sugar that he then handed off into our eager hands. Because it was a cloud of aerated sugar, each bite of it dissolved instantaneously like saccharine raindrops on our tongues.

These conjurors of cotton candy, touts exhorting we innocents to test our skills at their unwinnable games, even the operatives beckoning us to ride their Ferris wheel were all gypsies, travelers of back roads, and their traveling entertainments were attractive nuisances. Or so my mother said. She warned us to avoid them. Even though I was a girl, I, too, was excused from being polite to them and ordered not to respond to questions or comments they might direct to me. According to my mother these gypsies were dangerous, as was so much else within Marshall's environment like the animals that might bite us, the wild berries that might poison us, the trees we might fall out of. If I was born timid, a childhood echoing with Mom's dire admonishments made me more so. Thus, I was afraid to tempt the lurking evil by interacting with these so-called gypsies. For their part, since I wasn't the person holding the nickels and dimes to pay for what they had on offer, these dangerous gypsies ignored me.

But it was the horses and horse racing that held the greatest interest for me. Most horse races held during the fair were harness races run by Standardbred horses. Harness racing is distinguished by the horses' pulling a sulky, a light cart equipped with two bicycle wheels. The sulkies are steered by a driver rather than a jockey. For training and exercise, the horses pulled a jog cart, a sulky that was heavier and bulkier than the racing unit. The jog carts were what I usually saw in use at the fairgrounds throughout the months the fair wasn't in town.

Standardbred horses have longer bodies and shorter legs than Thoroughbreds and race at a specific gate, a trot or a pace. Trotters move their legs forward in diagonal pairs; pacers move their legs forward laterally. Although the harness races I witnessed at the Clark County Fair in 2013 were evenly split between pacers and trotters, I have read that pacing constitutes 80 to 90% of United States harness races. Infrequent horse racing viewers can most easily identify pacers by the hopples they often wear. Hopples, or hobbles, are the leather straps connecting the front and rear legs on the same side of the horse. The hopples don't cause a horse to pace but balance a horse's stride and aid in supporting a pacing gait at top speed. Since I was infatuated with horses and spent so much time visiting those stabled year round at the fairgrounds, I could distinguish trotters from pacers simply from the sound of their running hooves striking the dirt of the racetrack. Viewed head-on while they're racing, pacers look like they're rocking from side to side. Pacers and trotters never race against each other because pacers have a faster gate.

Almost all North American harness races are one mile. Since the circumference of the track at the fairgrounds is one half mile, the horses circle it twice counter-clockwise. A motorized starting gate, or mobile barrier, was utilized at Marshall. The horses lined up behind the hinged gate, which looked like a ladder extending from the side rear end of a slow-moving motor vehicle, that lead them up to the starting line. At that point, the wing of the gate folded up against the vehicle, which accelerated away from the horses and rightward to the outside rail. The horses swept towards the inner rail, maneuvered by their drivers into what they considered the best position to complete the racecourse circuit. The horses usually raced in two rows along the inner rail up to the homestretch where those shadowing the front-runners fanned out across the track if they had sufficient stamina, and they all surged forward in a furious sprint to the finish line.

At the time, I was in my typical little-girl-crazy-in-love-with-horses phase. I innocently enjoyed watching their kinetic power without ever seeing a horse suffer a devastating breakdown during a race, without being aware such tragedies even occurred. Now I pay more attention to thoroughbred racing where these equine disasters are frequent. Thanks to the Internet, we can now watch Go For Wand, Pine Island and Eight Belles break down in endless loops. We can witness Go For Wand and Eight Belles euthanized on the racetrack where they collapsed. The naïve child I was didn't know either that even Kentucky Derby winners and contenders were sold to rendering factories, as happened to Ferdinand, or suffered suspicious injuries requiring euthanasia as was Alydar's fate. Many authors and journalists in various equine-related media expressed suspicions that the insurance policy on Alydar was of greater worth to his owner than his potential as a breeding stallion.

The fair and the summer ended, as time requires of all things. The gypsies packed up their enticements and decamped. Just as I didn't know from whence they came, neither did I have any idea to whence they departed. Akin to their pink cotton candy, they materialized in Marshall at the tail end of July and then dissolved back into the wider world one week later. The farmers' families and the 4-H members gathered their livestock and produce; they gathered their accumulated blue, red, and green winning ribbons; and they returned to the season and weather driven cycle of their farm chores. The townsfolk males returned to their work-a-day jobs. The wives returned to the houses to which they were married. We children and teen-agers set aside the pursuits of summer and resumed our schoolwork and homework.

21

North Side School

I ATTENDED GRADES two through six at Marshall's North Side School. It must have acquired that name because it had been built north of Archer Avenue. There was also a South Side School, south of Archer Avenue, of course. North Side School was approximately five blocks from our house. There was no public transportation, and my parents weren't about to drive their healthy young children a measly five blocks. That meant my brothers and I walked to school just as we walked everywhere in Marshall. Granted, we didn't have to cross any heavily-trafficked roadways. Not even Archer Avenue on a Saturday when the farmers came into town could be honestly described as traffic-choked. We didn't have to pass through dangerous neighborhoods, rival gang territories, or public housing projects because Marshall had none of those. I remained ignorant of such contextual menaces until we moved back to Chicago when I was thirteen. My mother was surprised that the school district didn't cancel classes when we experienced our first heavy snowfall in which the accumulating snow climbed to my mid-calf. That still didn't convince her to drive us to school. Dad left the house too early to accommodate us, but it would never have occurred to me to even think of asking him for a ride anywhere.

I don't know when it occurred, but, like many older structures in the area, my school was razed. A new North Elementary School at a different location has replaced it. The North Side School of my elementary school years was a two-story fortress-like building of dark stone sited on one square block between Beech and Ash Streets and North Seventh and North Eighth Streets. The girl's entrance was on Beech Street, the same side of the building as the basement level girl's bathroom. Boys had their own entrance, and bathroom, on the opposite side of the building fronting Ash Street. Instead of the miles of cement and linoleum hallways lined with metal lockers, and the rooms filled with furniture of metal and fire-resistant materials of their contemporary models, the North Side School was almost entirely constructed of wood. The wood-paneled classrooms of the lower grades were arranged in the four corners of the first floor; upper grades were similarly situated on the second floor. Each classroom had its own attached wood-paneled cloakroom with black metal hooks for our coats and other cold weather gear. The floors throughout the classrooms and hallways were timber planks. In other words, we were learning our ABCs in a tinderbox.

Our rows of desks with their fold-up benches, bolted into the floorboards perpendicular to the teacher's substantial wood desk and podium, were also of wood with scrolled cast iron legs and with an inkwell for the ink fountain pens we didn't possess. We were restricted to writing with pencils. Some of the desktops displayed names or initials gouged into them by previous scholars. Just as all boys possessed BB guns, many of them were also equipped with pocket knives. I know at least one of my male classmates also carried a switchblade knife. He slashed the palm of his hand when the knife sprang open as he stuck his hands in his pockets. My best guess is that's the means by which some of our desks were branded.

Our progress through each grade could be physically tracked. We began in first grade on the first floor. Upon our successful completion of first grade, we rotated clockwise to the next classroom on the first floor for the next school year. We circled through the classrooms on the first floor before moving up to the circle of classrooms on the second floor for grades five and six. The fifth and sixth grades were sufficiently large enough for each to be split between two classrooms. On the second floor, our school experiences expanded to include descending the exterior metal fire stairs during fire drills. Whichever student had the good – or mis-fortune – to be seated nearest the fire door exit had to leap to his or her feet at the first jarring clang of the fire alarm, push the door open, and lead the rest of the class onto the black metal grill of the fire stairs as our accumulated weight dropped it to the ground. I remember how our sixth grade teacher, the red-haired Mrs. Irwin, laughed at the looks of relief washing over our faces as we stepped onto the steadfast earth of the playground. If we were in the first floor classrooms, we exited through the closest door, disregarding for that moment whether it was the girls' or the boys' entrance. In that manner, the school disgorged us onto the grass and dirt (real grass, real dirt, no cement) playground across which we marched in orderly lines to the public sidewalks encircling our school. Also new in sixth grade were individual metal desks and chairs that replaced the rows of wood desks with flip-up benches. We were measured in order to match us to a desk and chair of the appropriate height.

Nobody "different" attended North Side School. We were uniformly white and spoke English, even at home, a home that was presided over by a working father and a stay-at-home mother. The one distinction amongst us, and a visually imperceptible one at that, was whether we were town kids or farm kids. The farm kids were transported between the school and their homes by the commonplace yellow school bus. They were rousted out of bed earlier than us town kids to do chores, like milking their family cows and sloping the hogs, before the school bus picked them up in the morning. They were allowed to depart our classrooms five minutes ahead of the rest of us in order to line up at Beech Street for their bus back out into the countryside. Because the same group of Marshall's school age children progressed through the same school at the same time, the homogeneity of the student body continued into Marshall Junior High, and probably into Marshall High School as well. Students and their parents had no options. All seventh and eighth grade students attended Marshall Junior High, and there was also only one high school in town. Charter schools didn't exist. I can't remember that faith-based schools did either. Nobody was home-schooled. Our parents believed that, vis-à-vis our education, their job was parenting. It was for the schools and teachers to teach us.

In sixth grade I became aware of two students in my age group who were circumstantially different. Jerome had no mother. His grandmother was raising him. On Mother's Day in our sixth grade class, Mrs. Irwin read aloud an ode to mothers, which sounded like it might have been generated by a literary hack on retainer to Hallmark Cards. I think it was at a line similar to: "M is for the many ways she loves me," that Jerome crossed his arms across his desktop, hid his face in them and started sobbing. It was so unnerving that my memory ends right there at that image of Jerome's trembling back curved over his desk and the sound of his weeping. I believe Jerome's mother had passed away but not so long ago that he couldn't remember her. Neither my classmates nor I appreciated that our rendezvous with adulthood would turn all of us into motherless children.

The second dissimilar student in my sixth grade class was an overweight girl whose name I cannot recall. That her weight made her unlike the rest of her thirty-five classmates, and in fact, distinguished her from all of the approximately 280 children attending North Side School, reveals how American children have changed physically in the fifty-five years since I attended elementary school. A normal weight in the fifties was assigned based on gender, height and three possible body frame sizes. One's body frame size could be quickly calculated by measuring one's wrist. Since my wrist circumference is less than 5.5 inches, I would know that I have a small frame. Actuaries based these determinations on research of the mortality rates of insurance policy holders. According to their formula, this girl's weight exceeded the range of desirable weights for a tall female with a large frame.

Our height and weight were recorded on our report cards yearly. Mrs. Irwin determined our height from a tape measure attached to the classroom wall. Our weight was read from a, now vintage, analog scale that measured up to only 250 pounds. Mrs. Irwin chose students to help her with this process. One student announced your height when you stood up against the tape measure; a second student announced your weight when you stepped onto the scale. Mrs. Irwin recorded the numbers as they were called out. This whole procedure was carried out alongside the teacher's desk, at the front of the room, while class was in session. Your classmates had nothing better to do while this was occurring than stare at whoever was being measured and weighed. Homework was to be undertaken at home – in the most exact sense of the words at home, as was extracurricular reading. In any case, the atmosphere within the room charged as it was with anxiety, expectation, and possible embarrassment, precluded endeavors more challenging than staring at each other.

Mrs. Irwin did evidence some empathy towards my unnamed overweight classmate during this ritual. She weighed this girl last and read the scale herself without calling out any numbers. This, too, of course, emphasized my classmate's differentness and suggested there was something about her that polite people didn't discuss openly. Today, I can't picture this situation arising. Now we're sensitive to medical privacy, affliction of pain and suffering, and harmful effect. And presently we also use BMI (body mass index) instead of a desirable range of weight for gender and height. Hiding within our own homes, we can troll the Internet for calculators to determine our BMI sans judgmental witnesses. BMI compares an individual's weight status to that of the general population. From the BMI scale, we no longer derive healthy weights but a currently normal weight, which is a moveable target determined by overall population diversity, sedentary lifestyles, and fat acceptance attitudes. My classmate was simply born too soon to pass through sixth grade unremarked.

While I was in sixth grade, four new students enrolled in our school, two sets of twins both from the same family. Identical twins Judy and Julie joined my class. Twin Judy became the fifth girl in my class with the name Judy. It is unusual today to encounter any woman younger than sixty who is named Judy. Judy and Julie's identical twin brothers, Jimmy and Johnny, were David's age and in his class. In fact, they moved into a large home just north of the old Montgomery house. Remarkably, also living on North Second Street, were my best friend Karen's twin sisters, Linda and Judith (yet another Judy). The Denny family next door to them welcomed twin boys named Roger and Rodney into their family about the same time I was in sixth grade. A set of triplets named Martin, Melvin and Merwin attended one of the lower grades at North Side School. It sounds like parents of that era favored alliteration in the names of their multiples.

In every grade at North Side School, I was considered a good student. I always came to class with my homework assignments completed. I was intelligent enough to memorize most spelling lists and the multiplication table, as well as being able to sight-read stories from our reading books. My printing and Palmer style cursive handwriting when we graduated to that was legible. Given sufficient time and scratch paper, I could even satisfactorily complete most arithmetic problems, although it was understood that, as a girl, I would never be as adept at math as my brothers or the boys in my class. But I was too shy to raise my hand to answer questions in class, and I tended to be a daydreamer. If our classroom activities weren't sufficiently engaging, I might become so immersed in reading a storybook that I missed hearing questions directed to me by the teacher or the answers to tests graded in class.

I remember our outdoor activities more than the subjects we studied in class. North Side School appropriated one complete block. The land surrounding the building constituted our playground. Mature hardwood trees, not chain-link fences, lined the outer perimeter of the block. I don't know where in Marshall we could have even found any of the spindly, thornless honey locust trees with their jelly-bean size leaves that stretch along many miles of Chicago's landscape. When the abundant leaves cascaded from Marshall's trees in fall, we girls swept them, with our hands because the school didn't have rakes to dispense to students, into variegated patterns on the ground that we declared were houses. Our gold and russet leaf houses resembled blueprints drawn with autumn leaves instead of pen and ink. Breaks in the lines of gathered leaves indicated doors; rectangular leaf piles within forty-five degree angles represented beds.

We didn't have a swimming pool, gymnasium, or any other physical education center at North Side School. The dirt and trampled grass playground upon which our educational institution sat brooding served as gym and playing field. Physical education classes were the only occasions during which boys and girls played together. The PE teacher appointed team captains who then picked their team members from among their classmates. I hated PE; I hated the picking of teams. I was always one of the last chosen. In elementary school, not only was I timid and clumsy, I was the shortest girl in my class as well. I hated the games we played. I especially dreaded red rover. Two teams, hands joined, formed opposing lines. Team A would call out in unison, "Red rover, red rover, send Judy right over." I, or whoever from Team B was singled out, had to then run across the open interval between the lines and try to break through the conjoined hands of the other team. If you burst through that physical chain, you could select a person from Team A and bring them back with you to add to your team's line. If, however, you failed to penetrate your opponent's line, you were forced to join their team. This game was the only occasion when

I was likely to be chosen first, when my name was called to come over during red rover. The other team knew I couldn't breach their line; everybody knew I couldn't. No matter at which pair of clasped hands I threw myself, I only succeeded in nearly being decapitated because the line of students could raise their outstretched arms to the same level as my neck.

The playground was equipped with swings, teeter-totters, and hanging bars primarily for the first and second graders. Boys and girls played separately, instinctively rather than by outside dictate. We girls avoided the boys because they had cooties; the boys probably kept their distance from us for some similar reason. I don't know how the boys entertained themselves. Cliques of girls practiced sports cheers. I'm not sure how that arose since we never played organized competitive sports at those grade levels. In one cheer that I remember, one girl would hold onto a second's hand and pirouette in towards her and then away as we all chanted: "The door swings in, the door swings out. If South Side (South Side School) wins, we'll all pass out." At that point, the swinging girl would collapse backwards into the arms of the second girl. Supposedly a great rivalry existed between North Side and South Side Schools. I believe that supposition was totally hype and imagination. Both schools sent their students on to Marshall Junior High School, which contained our seventh and eighth grades. I never experienced or observed any disharmony or competitiveness between the two groups when we were eventually and inevitably conjoined at junior high.

We girls also jumped rope accompanied by chanted rhymes. After we moved back to Chicago, I discovered how elemental our rope skipping techniques at North Side had been. In Marshall, we knew nothing about jumping double-Dutch using two ropes turn-ing in opposite directions and with more than one jumper. We weren't aware of alternate feet, or speed-step jumping, in which the jumper, or skipper, jumps off the ground with alternate feet. This method can double the number of skips per minute. Nor did we know about double under in which the rope swings under the feet twice before passing over the head once; we certainly didn't know of triple and quad under. We were only familiar with the basic or easy jump in which both feet jump over the rope at the same time, and we only utilized one rope.

Our rhymes began when the skipper jumped in and ended when she (boys wouldn't be caught dead engaged in a sissy activity like skipping rope) skipped out. One of our rhymes went: "Ching, Ching Chinaman Miranda, here comes Karen in the door." At that point Karen would jump into the swinging rope just before it passed over her head. The group would continue chanting, "Karen is the one that we all like best, and we don't like Roslyn anymore." Roslyn, the original skipper, ran out the opposite side after the rope passed under her own and Karen's feet. I can't explain the opening words. None of us had ever encountered anyone of Chinese ances-try. Perhaps that was just one example of the unexamined xeno-phobia of midwestern small towns and the fifties.

Each grade also participated in one music class per week. Similar to our physical education class, it was elemental as to content and spartan with regards to equipment and facilities. Music class, real-ly a sing-along accompanied by piano, took place in a dimly-lit basement room furnished with a piano and rows of folding metal chairs. This room was not adorned in any way to make it seem like anything other than the room in a basement that it was, complete with a drain in the cement floor, wire mesh over the windows, and the furnace around the corner. The folding chairs were divided into two sections. We received an assigned seat within a section based on our vocal range. So, here again, most boys sat on one side of the room and most girls sat on the other side of the room. In simple unison, we sang selections from a songbook intended for children in elementary school. During the month of December, *America the Beautiful* and *Frère Jacques* were replaced by traditional Christmas carols. For us that did not include *I Saw Mommy Kissing Santa Claus* (too confusing for our immature minds) or *Santa Baby* à la Eartha Kitt (too suggestive).

Our so-called music room also served as our so-called lunch-room for those who weren't able to walk home for lunch. That group was primarily the farm kids. I almost always walked the five blocks home and back during our forty-five to sixty minute lunch hour. Occasionally I brought a lunch to eat at school, thereby turn-ing lunch into an adventure. As with much else that I remember from my Marshall years, we made do without realizing that's what we were doing. We lacked tables at which to eat our lunch. Nor were we allowed to reposition the folding chairs. We sat in them as they were arranged for our singing class and ate our lunches of peanut butter and jelly sandwiches, apples, carrot and celery sticks, and cookies from paper bags or lunch boxes that we balanced on our laps. A teacher took up her position on the piano bench to supervise us and to open the tops of stubborn thermos bottles for us. As the only male teacher, the physical education teacher was exempt from lunchroom monitoring duties. Watching six to twelve year old children eat lunch was not in his job description.

A marked constant of North Side School that I only noticed after we moved back to Chicago was the absence of behavioral and disciplinary issues despite class sizes of thirty to thirty-five youngsters or more. School personnel at that time had a free hand to physically discipline us, including hitting and slapping. If and when your parents discovered you had brought such chastisement down upon yourself at school, they blamed nobody else but you. If a teacher struck you, your patents were angry with you because they reasoned the teacher must have had just cause to resort to physical punishment. Parents didn't demand explanations, apologies, or policy changes from the teacher, principal, or school board. It never occurred to them to file a lawsuit. The universal message from all our parents was that, if we were disciplined at school, we would be punished twice as severely at home. Without a troublemaker in any class instigating mischief, the prevailing good behavior reinforced itself.

From North Side School I and every other child my age proceeded on to seventh and eighth grades at Marshall Junior High School. Marshall Junior High was a separate building adjacent to Marshall High School, the town's only high school. In junior high, we rotated through different classrooms to be taught by teachers who specialized in a single subject matter, unlike elementary school where we spent our entire school day in one classroom under the supervision of one teacher who taught all subjects. We began each school day in an assigned homeroom with our homeroom teacher, whom we might or might not have as a teacher for a specific subject later in the day. Each morning in our homeroom opened with a morning hymn and prayer broadcast over the public address system. This routine didn't seem remarkable to me when it was occurring. But when my latter-life Chicago and suburban class-mates heard of this practice, they assumed that I had attended a church-affiliated school. Marshall Junior High was a public school, but this was the conservative fifties in a conservative county whose largest religious affiliation was and still is the Southern Baptist Confession according to government census statistics. No student or parent ever questioned or protested this morning ritual nor did any student refuse to participate.

Similar to the Clark County Fair portending the end of summer and our return to school, May Day signaled the approaching end of the school year. May Day occurred on May 1st and seemed to be exclusive to my years in Marshall. To celebrate May Day, we children created handled baskets from construction paper. We picked small flowers, such as the lilies-of-the-valley that grew in our side yard and the violets that reappeared annually in the drainage ditches along Second Street, and arranged them in our handmade baskets. We hung these little flower-filled baskets on the door handles of our neighbors, rang their doorbells, and then darted away to hide nearby hoping to glimpse our neighbors' surprised delight. Our neighbors in Chicago and in the south suburb to which we later moved had never even heard of this early spring custom.

I did not attend Marshall High School as my father had because our family moved back to Chicago during the latter half of the year I was in eighth grade. There I completed eighth grade at a feeder school that sent its students on to Fenger High School, which is located in Chicago's Roseland community. My mother and my Aunt Eleanor, who was married to Mom's brother Leonard, both attended Fenger. However, I didn't attend Fenger either. My family moved to one of Chicago's southern suburbs immediately before I began high school where I attended a supposedly better school in a safer neighborhood. It was one of those stifling Levittown look-alike suburbs which, up to then, I had been spared from living in.

22

By Our Clothing You Shall ID Us

I THINK IT was the times, but at North Side School and Marshall Junior High we girls always wore pastel or plain white cotton blouses neatly tucked into our skirts, or we wore shirtwaist dresses. Hemlines always extended to just below our kneecaps. In cooler weather, a sweater might replace a blouse, or we wore cardigans. In winter, it was acceptable for us to wear flannel slacks under our skirts or dresses to and from school. Once at school, slacks had to be removed and hung in the cloakroom until we left the building. Our mothers dressed the same way.

When it came to underwear, it was unthinkable not to wear it but also unthinkable to let the world see that you were wearing it. If need be, we employed small safety pins to secure our undershirt and slip straps to the insides of our blouses. When we matured into them, we did the same with bra straps. If our slip sagged below the hem of our dress or skirt, we tried to roll it up a bit at the waist and cinched our belts tighter to keep it there.

When someone whispered to one of my classmates that her slip was peeking out below her skirt, she tried to brush aside her faux pas by repeating that era's saying, "I'm trying to catch a husband."

All of our underwear was unembellished white cotton from places like Sears, J.C. Penney or Montgomery Ward. Even if Jezebel lingerie had been available before 1957, the name alone would have convinced our mothers not to buy it for us. The most risqué underwear we may have worn would have been "weeklies," those packs of seven panties with the names of the days of the week embroidered on them.

It may be just as well my mother and her contemporaries did not live long enough to meet Dina, who was my roommate in the late sixties and early seventies. Dina shared with a group of us, "Realistically, ladies, do I look like I need a bra? I am so flat chested I have nothing to put into a bra. And I save money on underpants, too, by not buying them and then by not having to spend time or money washing them. So, I save time and money by simply not wearing underwear." Hearing that would have caused the heart of a fifties woman to decompensate. Or, alternatively, would have given her something to gossip about for practically forever.

Our mothers chose the Buster Brown shoes we all wore. Most girls sported Mary Janes, black or black patent leather flat shoes with a round toe box and a thin strap that buckled across the instep. Our other option was the classic saddleback oxford, a white lace-up shoe with a low heel and a wide strip of black leather over the instep, hence its name. Because I had flat feet and on the advice of the pediatrician, my mother refused to outfit me in anything but solid black lace-up Buster Brown oxfords. I don't know if that was supposed to cure them, but my arches are still as flat as the floor

I'm standing on unless I consciously flip up my toes for yoga poses. That simple action put an arch in your foot. Our socks were equally pedestrian, white cotton anklets. On special occasions, younger girls could dress up by wearing lace-edged anklets.

We may have lived in farm country, but we never wore blue jeans. Only farmers wore blue jeans. And we weren't farmers. We, including the farm kids, certainly didn't wear blue jeans to school, and girls didn't even wear slacks into their school classrooms. Nor did we wear blue jeans even to play in. Farm kids may have worn jeans to perform their chores. I know my father had a pair of jeans that he wore while working around the barn, pig lots, and hen yard. He may have also worn them during his workday at the poultry house. I have a snapshot of Uncle Lauf in blue denim bib overalls. He was wearing them over a white shirt and tie, which indicated to me that the picture must have been taken on a Sunday.

At that time, and in that place, only farmers wore blue jeans. Now blue jeans are the North American national uniform, although it's hard to fathom their popularity because they're too hot in summer and not warm enough in winter. When my husband and I first started traveling to foreign countries in the mid-eighties, we never packed blue jeans because that would have advertised to all who saw us that we were from the United States. We are as proud to be Americans as the staunchest Republican. But the citizens of some foreign countries, even our supposed allies, are not enraptured with America or Americans. Some people in those countries distinguish between the American people, whom they admire, and our government, which they abhor. In other locales, we stand in as representatives of our world bully government and are disrespected accordingly. But even as the cultures of some conquered nations have seduced their conquerors, elements of United States habits, such as its blue jeans, have infiltrated every continent. Everyone – even those who shouldn't – wear them. In more recent years, I have encountered women wearing blue jeans in Scotland, where it's so damp denim blue jeans never dry out, and in Indonesia, where the temperature is a humid 90 degrees every day.

23

Women's Work vs. Important Work, Which Is What Men Do

I LOVED TO simply sit and read, but my mother discouraged that. "You can sit inside and read all winter while you're in school," she advised me. "You read too much anyway. So go outside and play while you can. And besides, when you grow up, you won't have time to play, let alone sit down and read."

Her life as I observed it attested to that reality. Nothing she spent her days doing stayed done. She was always busy, ensnared in an unending and repeating cycle of mothering, cooking, and cleaning. Like the sun, she rose every morning to undertake variations of the same chores she had performed the preceding day but which time and family had undone by sundown. However and despite her advice to me, she also enjoyed immersing herself in the alternative world of some author's fictitious narrative. Some of my fondest memories of that time are the precious few nights that Mommy let me sit up past my customary bedtime and read with her.

Reflecting on them, I can see those nights again as if I were looking backwards through the wrong end of a spyglass. Mom prepared cups of hot cocoa for the two of us the way it was done back then, mixing together cocoa powder, milk, and sugar while heating those ingredients in a pan on top of the stove. She carried the cups, emitting the exquisite aroma of chocolate and in which two marshmallows floated, into the front room on a tray which she set down on a hassock close to hand. We sipped cocoa as we sat together on the sofa absorbed in our books as the house sank into stillness around us.

My father didn't like to see me sitting around inside reading either. If he chanced upon me reading a book, he would sarcastically snap at me, "That's right, just sit there on your fat, lazy ass with your nose in a book and let Mom do all the work."

The only response allowed to me was – silence. Shut my book and my mouth, and stand up and do something that females were supposed to do. He never helped Mom, of course. "All the work" meant housework, childcare, and cooking, all of which were women's work. Dad's contribution to the economic partnership of their fifties-style marriage was holding down a job and bringing home a paycheck every Friday. When he returned home at the end of his workday, it was the end of his working day. Mom was on duty every hour of every day. I don't remember anyone around me questioning this arrangement.

But what that meant for me was, summers and vacations notwithstanding, I also helped Mom with household chores and helped care for the baby, the baby during those years being Gordon who was eight years younger than me. I hung the laundry out to dry on the clotheslines, two of which extended parallel to and almost the full length of the north side of the house, and one running on an oblique angle westward a few steps from the back porch to a post near a corner of the hen yard. I don't remember our having a clothes dryer although surely we must have. But Mom and many other housewives considered it preferable to hang the family laundry in the fresh air and sunshine of the outdoors to dry. In winter, we hung laundry in the inside back porch and along one side of the dining room. The dining room was largely unused except for holiday dinners and my parents' weekend card parties. When the winter cold saturated our drafty house, the baby's diapers were hung in the only place they would dry, by the furnace in the basement.

I ironed the laundry as well. And we ironed everything. No-iron garments were not available yet. Mom and I and all females at that time wore cotton blouses, skirts, and dresses which needed to be ironed. I also ironed my three brothers' shirts and slacks because ironing was a girl's job. I ironed tablecloths, which we used every day at every meal; napkins, handkerchiefs, pillowcases, and probably the bed sheets, too. We changed the bed linens on five beds every week. And sometimes as often as daily on the baby's crib and on Brad's bed because he wet the bed every night. I have no proof to offer but maybe every housewife was that way at that time. I know my mother was a fanatic about her home presenting a perfect appearance. In the fifties and before she sank into alcoholism, she thought such things mattered. I even had to iron my father's boxers. He liked the smooth, soft texture of ironed cotton boxers. At least we weren't expected to starch those. Laundry starch could be concocted by mixing cornstarch into a bucket of water. Starching put crisp creases into shirtsleeves, for instance, and helped clothing resist wrinkling. Its proponents claimed that it also kept clothes cleaner because sweat, skin debris, dirt, and other grime attached to the starch rather than the material. Starch supposedly made ironing easier but I can confirm from experience that it also may leave behind a residue.

And of course, since there always seemed to be a baby in the house, we spent a lot of time changing and washing diapers. Pampers were launched in 1961, so we were dealing with reusable cloth diapers. Mom insisted that excrement-filled diapers be swished in a flushed toilet a time or two then wrung out into the toilet, after which dirty diapers were collected in a covered diaper pail, dispersing an effluvium of ammonia, until such time as they could be washed. I strongly resisted touching them at all. In exasperation, and as tears ran down my cheeks, my mother screamed at me, "When you grow up, you'll be sticking your hands in shit worse than this, young lady!" On most occasions, I wouldn't hesitate to blatantly lie in order to avoid having my mother hit me or cause her to raise her voice. Despite that, my aversion to the repugnant puree of malodorous brown in the triple or double folds of soggy cotton prevailed over my fear of punishment, whether physical or verbal. If I changed the baby before Mom woke up in the morning and after Dad left for work, I often threw the soiled diaper under their bed. The baby's crib was in my parents' room until he graduated to a twin bed in the upstairs bedroom.

Even if it chanced to be summer vacation, I still helped Mom make the beds every morning, fold laundry, vacuum the area rugs in the front room and downstairs bedroom, dust furniture and the wood floors. I washed the kitchen and bathroom floors on my hands and knees with a cloth rag and bucket of diluted Pine Sol. That's the way it was done before Swiffer Sweepers and WetJets. But there were more hours in a summer day than Mom could fill with household chores that she trusted me to perform unsupervised.

Often enough she told Dad and her in-laws, "It's easier for me to just do it myself than try to teach one of the kids and then have to stand over them to make sure they do it right." That was how I managed to immerse myself so completely in both Marshall's physical landscape and its public library's books.

Dad and other men, meanwhile, had real jobs for which they were paid real money unlike women who were paid in love and kisses. Men made a living for their families, and their families made the living worthwhile. Well, that was the prevailing aphorism. With some exceptions, such as farm families, the men disappeared for approximately forty hours a week to do or produce we didn't know or understand what. What we were supposed to understand, though, was that whatever they were doing, not only made them money, but also made them important. For that reason, men's care and comfort took precedence over that of women and children.

A perennial question in Marshall was: Where have all the young folks gone? Just as there were no universities or vocational schools in Marshall, neither were there enough industries to soak up each year's entire high school graduating class. I can think of only two major manufacturers in the area at that time. One of those was where the father of my best friend Karen worked. He always seemed to be dressed nicely, in a shirt and tie rather than uniform-like work clothes, which led me to believe he worked in an office of the plant that manufactured lighting fixtures. But I never knew more than that about that business or Mr. Kannemacher's role there.

The only other significant employer in the vicinity was Velsicol Chemical Corporation's Marshall plant, which was located one mile north of Marshall on Route 1. Sometimes we had to shut all the windows on the north side of our house in an attempt to block out the foul-smelling odor carried from the plant by the northerly wind. As a youngster I had been told that Velsicol made "bug juice". Now everyone with Internet access is able to inform themselves about Velsicol's products and processes because of its status as an EPA (Environmental Protection Agency) superfund toxic clean-up site. Marshall's public library is the repository for its written records. When my husband, who is a civil engineer, and I drove past the former Velsicol property, he immediately recognized it as a superfund clean-up site. He was tipped off by the engineered composite low-permeability cap which had been installed on-site and re-vegetated.

Velsicol had been producing a variety of resins, solvents, and rubber extenders derived from petroleum by-products since the mid 1930s. Beginning in 1946, the plant also began manufacturing chlordane, a synthetic toxic compound used as an insecticide. In 1965, an injection well was installed on Velsicol's acreage for the disposal of waste water and storm run-off. Prior to that, process waste water was discharged from the plant without treatment. A second well was installed in 1973. In 1979, Velsicol withdrew from the resin market. Chlordane remained its sole product after 1980. The EPA classifies chlordane as a probable human carcinogen. Accordingly, it cancelled the use of chlordane on food crops in 1978, and in 1988 it cancelled all approved uses of chlordane in the United States.

Velsicol ceased manufacturing operations at the Marshall plant in 1988. The ground water, sediment, and on-site soil are contaminated with volatile organic chemicals (VOC) and pesticides. The sediment and soil are also contaminated with cadmium. The engineered cap that my husband pointed out to me covers the twenty-two acre retention pond which had contained the majority of waste solids and sludge generated over the plant's lifetime

I wasn't aware of anyone at that time who appeared to be concerned about Velsicol's operations or products. Those of us who lived within range of Velsicol's odors and discharges were ignorant of any harm which we might be incurring. Regardless, even when possible and certain hazards are general knowledge, people can be induced to risk working anywhere if the knowledge of potential ill effect or danger is offset by sufficient incentives.

My brothers and I probably had a concrete grasp of most aspects of our father's work because we could observe him performing it. Dad and his uncle Lauf operated the poultry and egg business that Lauf's father, my paternal great-grandfather Pop who lived next door to us, had developed. When Pop decided at age 74 to retire, he turned his by then thriving business over to his youngest son Lauf. I don't know how Dad became incorporated into this family business venture, but I'm sure that being the son of Pappy who was Lauf's older brother counted for a lot. I never knew either what Dad's business relationship was to Uncle Lauf, whether he was a co-owner or employee. I suspect it was the latter since Dad brought little to the table but his family connection and his physical capability.

I wasn't sophisticated enough then to recognize that Dad and Uncle Lauf were aggregators and that the poultry house in Marshall was a small scale food hub. I'm not certain that anyone at that time perceived of their business and their role in the local food chain in those terms. Dad bred his three sows and sent the shoats they produced each year to market. We also raised a flock of no more than three-dozen white leghorn hens that we sold live locally after they matured. There were no factory farms around us. No one owned thousands, let alone hundreds, of chickens, swine, or cattle. Both Dad and Uncle Lauf drove around to the family-owned farms dispersed throughout the surrounding countryside collecting poultry, eggs, and raw cow's milk. These were aggregated at the poultry house then conveyed and resold by Dad and Uncle Lauf to commercial markets in Chicago and Indianapolis. Dad and Uncle Lauf relieved farmers from marketing and distribution chores and supplied the closest large pool of food shoppers.

What we called the poultry house was an old-fashioned storefront located on the northeast corner at the intersection of South Fifth Street and Archer Avenue across the street from the Clark County Courthouse Square. The square was so named for the Clark County Courthouse erected there in 1904, and to this day it occupies the entire block from Archer Avenue south to Locust Street and from South Fifth to South Sixth Streets west to east. The City Bandstand was erected in 1929 on the northeast corner of the square. The Marshall City Band still performs free concerts at the bandstand at 8:00 p.m. on Friday evenings from June through August.

Based on its stamped tin ceiling, I judged the poultry house to be of a comparable vintage to the courthouse. Its main room was expansive and contained most of the equipment pertinent to the business. The egg-grading machine was pushed up against the back wall and opposite the windows fronting onto the street. The egg-candling apparatus was placed conveniently to the left of the egg-grader. Forward of them, closer to the center of the room, was the wood-burning cast iron potbelly stove. Closest to the front door and the street-side wall of windows was a red Coca Cola vending machine, and, as I vaguely recall, some kind of desk and a wooden counter. In a small dim side room, crates, each holding twelve dozen eggs, were stacked awaiting delivery to the Chicago or Indianapolis markets. Also behind this cavernous first room was a loading dock of sufficient size to accommodate the business' flatbed truck.

Some evenings, Mom was pressed into giving Dad a hand at the poultry house. On such occasions, David, Brad, and I spent our evening with them. We helped by staying out of Dad's way. There was no overhead light; the blue light bulb in the candling device and the fire in the potbelly stove sufficed for my parents to clean, candle, grade, and pack eggs. As twilight surrendered to deeper dusk, my interest and energy likewise waned. I wilted into the ancient office swivel chair to observe all else. Mice scurried furtively around the room's dusky perimeter. My parents' silhouettes cast upon the far wall dipped and swayed like dancers cued by the rhythmic, mechanical clack-clacking orchestra of the egg-grading machine.

My mother stood to the left cleaning dirt and straw from the eggs with a hand-held brush similar to the ones we use to buff our manicured fingernails. Next she candled the polished eggs. Candling is a method of passing an egg in front of a bright light source to see imperfections through the shell, such as cracks in the shell, blood spots or an unacceptably large air sac. In our case, Mom pressed the more pointed end of the eggs up to the port-hole in a contraption that resembled a metal can containing a lit blue light. This technique is so called because the original sources of light were candles. Lastly, Mom laid the blemish-free eggs on the slanted ramp that fed them into the egg-grading machine, also called an egg-sorting machine.

The eggs rolled down the ramp in single file and onto the moving bar of the egg-grader. Cantilever weights allowed each egg to be released into the right chute, or trough, depending upon its weight. Dad stood to Mom's right picking the eggs up out of the chutes and depositing them into cardboard filler flats, or trays, a dozen eggs to a flat. The flats were then stacked in crates, a dozen flats to a crate. These filled crates were stored in the side room until Dad or Uncle Lauf trucked them into the big city. This journey was for the white eggs only. Supposedly, city folks didn't like the appearance or the spicier taste of brown eggs. I always thought this notion that brown eggs were spicier was a fallacy. Since the white eggs went to market, we always ate only brown eggs at home. Nowadays I can buy brown eggs, which still taste the same to me as white eggs, at Whole Foods Market where they presently cost more than all but the omega-3 white eggs.

My mother cursed whenever she broke an egg in her hand while buffing it. She would stride over to the potbelly stove, yank open its upper door and shake the slimy, crushed remnants off her hand then slam the door shut again and return to her post. Just as our egg-candler and egg-grading machine were primitive in comparison to what is currently offered commercially, our potbelly stove was antique. Its defining feature was its bulbous center that rounded out from narrower top and bottom sections. It was made of cast iron, even the two doors on the front. The top door was large enough to load in wood or coal. The smaller bottom door was used to remove ashes. Since Mom was not nimble-fingered enough to avoid breaking the occasional egg, Dad judged us children to be that much more likely to break significantly more of those ovoid representations of our bread and butter. So, my brothers and I spent such rare evenings at the poultry house unobtrusively entertaining ourselves but nowhere near any eggs or anything else breakable.

Like a British Redcoat soldier,,the red Coca Cola vending machine stood close to the front door and windows of the poultry house. For five cents, it dispensed contoured green 6.5 ounce bottles of Coke. Those bottles of Coke were priced at five cents for seventy years, partly because the vending machines only accepted a single nickel and did not return change. Nor would it have been a simple operation to replace all the vending machines spread throughout every state. Recently I saw the same or similar six ounce bottles of Coke available at a Candyality store for $1.75. And I see that vintage Coke and other soda-dispensing machine restorers and vendors have taken up residence on the Internet. I never troubled my mother to ask for a nickel to buy myself a Coke. The answer was always no. I was too frightened of my father to ask him for anything, including money to waste on carbonated water and syrup that rotted my teeth. At home my brothers and I never drank anything but milk and water. In summer, we were also allowed to drink Kool-Aid.

Housework for women, real and important work for men, and no work available for Marshall High School's graduating seniors who weren't baccalaureate-bound: that was the 1950s world of work in Marshall.

24

If I Ask Why

I WAS PROMPTED one afternoon to ask my mother, "Mom, do I have any good qualities?"

"Well, of course you do," she assured me.

"Like what?"

She paused, then told me, "I can't think of any right now."

Then she dismissed me on some errand or otherwise waved me away. She didn't even throw out some random obvious characteristic, like the fact that I was quiet and obedient. Nor did she spew forth some attribute common to all the world's little girls, such as wanting to please their mothers. Apparently I didn't have so much as one positive virtue in my mother's estimation. She didn't even trouble herself to fabricate some sort of lie to pacify me.

<hr/>

I was so enraptured by horses that I tried to talk my mother into buying one for me. We would see sway-backed, bone-spavined candidates for the glue factory at the Clark County Fair wearing For Sale signs with price tags of five or ten dollars.

"Only five dollars, Mom. We could afford that. I could pay you back out of my allowance. " I sporadically received a twenty-five cent weekly allowance. Truthfully though, Mom and Dad saw no reason to give my brothers or me an allowance at all. They bought us whatever they deemed we needed. If something was unafford-able, it was probably also unnecessary. As far as teaching us how to manage money, they did that by yelling at us not to waste food, hold the refrigerator door open, or leave the light on when we exit-ed a room. Still, it was my best bargaining chip.

"That horse is only five dollars, Mom."

"It's not just the first five dollars you pay for a horse," my moth-er explained. "Then you need a stable for it."

"We could put it in a stall in the barn."

"The barn is for your father's hogs. It just isn't an appropriate space for a horse. And you couldn't leave it out in the pig lots in the cold and snow in winter. Besides that, you have to feed it every day. That costs more money. And then you need a bridle and saddle. The cost of owning a horse is more than the original five dollars you pay for it today," my mother patiently spelled out in her opposing arguments.

I was subdued by her reasoning. She was able to convince me that horses selling for five dollars don't, in fact, cost the buyer a mere five dollars. Customarily neither Mom nor Dad saw any rea-son to explain their dictates. If my brothers or I dared ask "why?" their answer was usually always, "because I said so, that's why." I could count on two fingers the number of discussions my mother engaged me in about why I could or could not do or have some-thing. That was one of them.

More typical was my mother telling me not to hang around the horse barns at the fairgrounds. "But why not?" I asked.

"Because I said so. That's no place for young ladies."

"But why not? What's wrong with going to look at the horses?"

"You heard me. Because I said so, that's why. I told you once, and I'm not going to tell you again. Stay away from there."

So I would sneak over to the horse barns at the fairgrounds without mentioning where I had been. I was infatuated by the strength and grace, even the pungent odor, of the hulking beasts that I was able to approach so closely that I could lay a tentative palm upon a velvet muzzle or suffer my face to be stung by the swish of a coarse black tail. I was too bashful to speak at length with the old men with deeply bronzed and seamed faces and hands that I encountered at the stables. Instead I watched as they breezed the Standardbreds pulling a jog cart around the track, and then walked their blanket-draped charges until the horses' flanks were cool to the touch. I plucked white and red clover out of the greensward between the playground equipment and the animal barns to offer to the horses. This was the same open landscape where the gypsies set up their booths and Ferris wheel each year during the week of the county fair.

My mother was too reticent to explain why it was acceptable to play on the swings, slide, and merry-go-round at the fairgrounds with my brothers, cousins, and friends but not why I should avoid solitary visits to the few horses stabled there with their caretakers throughout the warmer months. Since I was not informed what I was supposed to be on guard against, I was forced to learn empirically.

One or another of the weathered men at the horse barns had on various occasions set me in the seat of an unhitched sulky or up on a horse's back. One afternoon, one of them invited me into a horse's box stall. Having entered it, I found myself sandwiched between the horse and him, and he was blocking the stall's sliding door. He wrapped his arms around me from behind and cupped the pre-teen bulbs of fat that passed for my breasts in his hands.

"How do you like that?" he asked. As nearly as I can recall that's what he said because my mind became a white hole of shock. My mother had never discussed inappropriate touching or bodily privacy with me.

All I can remember saying to that man is, "That's not nice."

He dropped his hands and stepped away. I immediately left and rode my bike back home. I didn't tell my parents. I was afraid of what they would do to me. I knew that incident was entirely my fault. If I hadn't been where I had been told repeatedly not to go, I wouldn't have been subjected to the sort of attention from him that I didn't expect or want.

So, thereafter, I understood the perils I might encounter at the horse barns, but I still lacked any idea what unspeakable harm my mother imagined the gypsies with their carnival caravan or strangers offering me candy or car rides would perpetrate upon me. She never could bring herself to clarify. I believe she sincerely believed that I would be safe from whatever ills she didn't explicitly describe, and that the adamant unexplained orders she issued would ward off the demons of the real world, even if those that infected her imagination remained in residence.

***

"Don't get married right out of high school like I did," my mother advised me. However, she never counseled me as to what alternative I might otherwise pursue. She had worked for one year after high school as a telephone operator then married at the age of eighteen. As a teen-ager, I hadn't yet perceived that my mother was cognitively unable to formulate anything else I might do with my life due to her own circumscribed life experiences.

One afternoon my mother and I encountered Doris, the older sister of one of my classmates, in a retail store. Doris worked at the store part time in the afternoon and on weekends as a sales clerk. Doris and I exchanged comments about my fast approaching junior high school graduation. My mother informed Doris, "Pretty soon Judy will be working at a counter next to you."

I told my mother again when we left the store as I had told her in the past. "I want to go to college."

If she hadn't made it clear to me previously, my mother then explained my future. "For what? Why waste money on something you'll never need? Being a wife and mother doesn't require a college degree."

It felt to me like my mother was basically saying, "Don't be in a rush to get married but don't expect to do anything else with your life except get married."

In the fifties, however, my parents weren't alone in expressing that sentiment. Even my school's guidance counselors counseled me that men were more in need of a college education because they would have a family to support. If women worked outside the home at all, it was for pocket change or to find a husband if they didn't already have one, and only for a year or two until they did marry.

Because of that prevailing conviction, my parents had always assumed that David would continue on to college. And he did proceed directly from high school to the University of Illinois at Urbana-Champaign with my parents' blessings and money, and five scholarships. Not only had Mom and Dad discouraged me from applying for college admission, but they also refused to provide their personal economic data that would have enabled me to apply for any financial assistance. David repaid my parents' bias by flunking out his first semester. I glowed with vindictive pleasure when I learned of his failure.

For many years I remained bitter that my parents, through their attitude and actions, thwarted my pursuit of a college degree. The variance between my parents' convictions and my yearning was made more painful when I compared my situation to that of my Uncle Leonard and my cousins CeeCee and Valerie. Their situation was the mirror opposite of my own. Uncle Leonard wanted nothing more for his girls than to provide them with a college education. They, on the other hand,,had no interest whatsoever in college; they wanted jobs and their own spending money, and not four years from now but the sooner the better.

<hr>

I never wanted to be my mother. I was obsessed with obtaining a college education; I almost didn't even care what subject it might be in. And I wanted a career, one that paid cash and respect, not a thankless, repetitive regimen exchanged for love and affection. Whatever my mother told me I should do, I endeavored to do the opposite. I made every effort to ensure that my life would be the exact opposite of the way my mother lived. Mom told Mammoo, "That Judith Ann is so stubborn." When it came to a college degree and paid employment, I was stubborn. Yet I gained what I wanted and more than I expected.

It took seven years, but I worked my way through undergraduate school to earn a BA in March of 1969. Thirteen years later, by combining savings, a fellowship, and an off-campus night-shift job, I completed an MS degree. In spite of that, my unresolved resentment hindered my emotional equilibrium. It was my husband who pointed out that I should be proud of myself, "You overcame adversity, became a productive and decent human being, traveled solo to a foreign country, and supported yourself while obtaining two college degrees." Only when I accepted the veracity of his observations, did my resentment start to fade. My rancor had impacted my parents not one whit. No matter who might have been at fault, if fault were to be assessed, the problem now existed in my mind and, thus, only I could correct it. I could remain mired in a poisonous stew of negativity, or I could acknowledge that I had the inner resources to pursue what I wanted. I didn't need someone else to pass me second-hand achievements. I had been able to recreate myself. I had valid justification to be prideful. I wanted to be happy, so that is the path I chose.

Some people, in fact, a great many people apparently are convinced that we planned our lives before we were born. They also believe that we choose the circumstances of our birth. Robert Schwartz, a self-styled past life and between lives regression therapist and author expounds on these beliefs in his two best-selling books *Your Soul's Plan*[9] and *Your Soul's Gift.*[10] According to the advocates of this belief system, I chose Bill and Elaine as they, likewise, chose me because we had lessons to learn from each other. Together we choreographed our lives before we lived them for the purpose of advancing our spiritual growth.

9. Robert Schwartz, *Your Soul's Plan* (Berkley, CA: Frog Books, 2007, 2009).
10. Ibid, *Your Soul's Gift* (Chesterland, OH: Whispering Winds Press, 2012).

I think, in fact, my mother admired me for the little part of my adult life that she did witness. She wanted to know everything I was about: what classes I was attending, what kind of work I performed, what places I traveled to. I was mindful of being her eyes and ears, her brain and stomach in the world. I intuited that I was living my life for her as much as for myself. If my mother had lived to see all that I did accomplish, I think she would be proud of me.

25

Headache: People and Places Well Intentioned

THE PAIN IS not who I am, but throughout most of my life it has prescribed and proscribed my activities. Since my preteens, my life has been periodically interrupted by anywhere from two days to two weeks of excruciating pain, like a railroad spike driven laterally down through the left side of my head, and accompanied by nausea, vomiting, sensitivity to light, and inability to sleep or focus my thoughts. In 1983, at the age of thirty-eight, I was finally and officially diagnosed with migraine without aura, tension-type headaches, and chronic daily headaches by Seymour Diamond, M.D., then director of the Diamond Headache Clinic in Chicago and founder of the National Headache Foundation (NHF).

I remember the first severe headache I experienced. It was mid-afternoon of a summer day during a season the farm news and weather radio station had characterized as drier than normal. I was running barefoot through the grassy stubble edging the faintly discernible gravel road between the house and the barn to join David and Brad in our plastic wading pool. Instead of placing it by the house under the shade of the weeping willow tree's umbrella of slender trailing branches, Mom had put the pool in the sun-soaked crook of the gravel path where it twisted around the barn. In that treeless, unshaded, unprotected spot, she could fill our pool with the hose at the barn. The landscape through which I ran shimmied and blanched in the fierce light. Then the sledgehammer of pain slammed down upon the crown of my head bringing me to a blinded staggering stop.

I told my mother that I had a terrible headache. She spun around, looming over me like a menacing thunderhead. She raised her right fist and her voice. "You have no right to have a headache!" she screamed at me. "You're just a kid."

I don't know what I did after hearing her say that. Cry? Vomit? Shut up and sit down like the good little girl everyone always said I was? Any memory of my response that day has vaporized, as a droplet of water on North Second Street's sidewalks would have.

But that was just the first day in a saga of discomfort and disability. My mother was no more sympathetic on any day thereafter that I experienced a headache. She yelled at me twice more when I admitted I had a headache. Her reaction didn't drive away my headaches. Instead, I stopped talking about them. I silently carried on as well as I could. I gritted my teeth against the nausea, shaded my eyes from the light, and tried to avoid any movement that would jar lose the railroad spike of pain cleaving the left side of my head.

Nor was there any sympathy to be had in the adult world I encountered after leaving my parents' house. Employers and co-workers couldn't understand why something as inconsequential as a headache would keep me from holding up my share of the workload. So, I didn't mention my head to them either and attempted to conceal the distracting storm of torment boiling within my skull. If they perceived me to be periodically moody and inefficient, they could snicker that I must be "on the rag" or that "after all, that's how girls behave."

Doctors, likewise, brushed me off, told me to take two aspirins and not to call again unless I had an illness that warranted their important time and attention. I screwed up my courage and presented myself to a women's clinic staffed by all female doctors. Their doctor cheerfully prescribed: "Jogging. The best thing for you is to take up jogging. I go jogging every morning, and I can tell you it works wonders." By then I was ingesting one hundred Excedrin every week, and my headaches were so severe I couldn't lift my head off my pillow during the course of one. Merely thinking of leaping out of bed every morning at 5:00 a.m. to run a mile and back made my head hurt and my stomach heave. The only exception I made to complete withdrawal to a cold, dark bedroom was when I forced myself to show up for my job.

I swore off doctors until, not only my exploding head, but also the searing pain of chronic ulcers caused by my aspirin intake impelled my husband to plead with me to consult an internist and the headache specialist Dr. Diamond. Doing so brought me relief but also lodged me on the ongoing treadmill of medication adjustments, specialist referrals, and endoscopies. Nonetheless, all of those are easier to bear than the unrelenting physical misery that put my life on hold up to four times a month.

Despite my own years of pain from chronic headaches, and despite the emotional turmoil my mother's reaction caused me, I unconsciously soaked up her attitude. My own ability to empathize with the ills of even those dearest to me was tarnished. Contempt was my immediate uncensored reaction to the friends who complained of their aching back because of their spinal stenosis or near immobility from osteoarthritic knees. My husband brought this to my attention when he entreated me, "Don't snap at me. I didn't choose to have a headache."

Little by little, as imperceptibly as growing grass, the migraineur's journey did enlarge my understanding. Even the child I had been could see that no one gave my mother any sympathy or support no matter what headache or heartache she suffered. And now I can appreciate how that deficit rendered her incapable of empathy towards me. This was just one more situation for which she lacked the material and emotional resources to help me.

If I could ever contact her again, I wouldn't demand that she make amends for failing me in this, too. Ultimately, there is nothing that she did or that she failed to do that has caused me irreparable harm. Perhaps, my mother yet lingers in the bardo, the Tibetan Buddhist indeterminate, transitional state of existence between death and rebirth. Were I to die forthwith and were I to find her awaiting me in that interval between re-embodiments, I no longer require her apology. Rather, I would sit with her in silent sorrow because she lived her short life with insufficient love – even from me.

26

Advice My Mother Gave Me

1. Always wear clean underwear in case you get hit by a car and are taken to the emergency room.

2. Always carry an extra dime in your purse. In case your date gets fresh with you, you will be able to call home for someone to pick you up. (Obviously a long time ago when you could find pay phones in public spaces and telephone calls cost only a dime. This was also before everyone, including first graders, had personal hand-held electronic devices.)

3. You have to finish all the food on your plate because of the starving children in India and/or China. (Those Indian and Chinese children must have been able to gain pleasure and sustenance vicariously from what I was eating half a world away. Upon comparing childhood experiences later in life with co-workers, I discovered this was near universal advice. The African American had to eat for the starving children in Africa, the west European Jew for the starving children in the Polish ghetto, the Hong Kong émigré for the starving children in China.)

4. Eating carrots will help you see in the dark, and you will never have to wear glasses. (I ate the carrots but have been wearing glasses since I was a high school sophomore. I had to pay for them myself from money I earned baby-sitting for the neighborhood children. Even by then I had already given up believing that I might ever receive help from my parents for anything beyond the minimum that would keep me alive. They didn't have to fear charges of child abuse or neglect because I had no idea interventionists exited. And, in fact, maybe they didn't at that time. I had also already given up believing that anyone in the larger world would ever help me either.)

5. Eating the bread crust and heels will make your hair curly. (So far, it's not working for me.)

6. Drinking coffee and tea will stunt your growth. (If I hadn't started drinking two to four cups of instant coffee a week when I was twenty-one, I would be six-and-a-half feet tall today. No doubt about it.)

7. Eating sugar will give you worms. (What looks like grains of sugar must be worm eggs that hatch when they enter your stomach. By the way, Mother, what does sugar do to your teeth?)

8. Boys don't like girls who reveal that they're smart. So play dumb, polite but dumb. (Most teen-age boys I met seemed more interested in what was between my legs than what was between my ears. That seems to indicate that my mother wasn't half dumb.)

9. Be polite at all times to all people, especially men. There are some exceptions, such as gypsies and strangers offering you candy or a ride in his car. If a man tries to yank you into a dark alley intent on raping you, it is acceptable to resist but in a polite and lady-like manner.

10. Don't get married at a young age.

11. There's no good reason for girls to attend college. You're going to be a housewife and mother. You don't need a college degree for that. By the way, how come you don't have a boyfriend already?

12. Never accept Dutch treat dates. A male should always pay for the pleasure of your company. And that's all you should give him until he marries you. (The fifties solidified the sexual double standard and made women responsible for men's sexuality. Received wisdom of the fifties was that a male would only go as far as a female would let him.)

13. Never take candy from a stranger and never accept rides from strangers. (Said when we lived in a town with a population of 3,000 people, and we were related to half of them.)

14. The reason I have to do or refrain from doing, or can have or can not have something is because she said so, that's why.

Even as a youngster, I recognized that if my brothers or any other male behaved in the manner that was expected of me— passive, unambitious, deceitful, and expecting others to protect and support me — they would have been regarded with contempt. But nobody else would admit that these characteristics were socially-imposed gender stereotypes.

Then as a young adult, if I suggested to women that it was not desirable for us to live as moochers dependent on a man to pay our way through life, they were puzzled as to why I would think there was anything wrong with such a lifestyle. I argued that women should pursue an education beyond high school as well as a decent paying career, establish a credit history in their own names, and, in fact, retain their maiden names. I pointed out that women who could support themselves and who controlled their own money could equalize the balance of power in a relationship with a man. Most other women thought I was crazy for not wanting to be taken care of while I failed to understand why they wanted to abdicate control over their own lives. The strongest desire of my whole life was, is, and always had been to be free, and I followed every path that I thought could take me there. For a long time I didn't understand that for many women freedom isn't free, it's an idea too scary to pursue.

27

What Was I Thinking?

MY MOTHER ADMITTED to me, "Daddy (Pappoo) always favored Leonard over me." She said this seriously, unselfconsciously, with a straight face.

I was speechless. She had treated me the same way Pappoo had treated her. She always favored David. In sharing this observation with me, she revealed no awareness that she had related to me, her only daughter, in the same manner as she, also an only daughter, had been related to by a parent. She perceived herself to have suffered life-long second-class status in her father's eyes, but she never examined that relationship and how devalued it made her feel. She never gained any understanding that she could leverage to expand her consciousness. Parents always have a favorite child, but they think we don't realize that.

⚜

My kindly Mammoo, who relayed information to my brothers and me that my parents wouldn't have broadcast, told me when I was about eight or nine years old, "During the Depression, your father's parents sent him to live on the farm," – most likely with Pop and Mom though that wasn't specified. "They did that so they could be sure he would have enough to eat. But, instead, that made him feel like they were rejecting him."

I remembered that incidental fact about Dad but didn't understand its import until half a lifetime later. I lacked the mental awareness then that I have painfully acquired over the intervening years. Just like my father, I would have to accuse myself of also bowing to the tyranny of unwarranted assumptions. I spent my elementary school years assuming my father was an adult. Prevailing conventions lead me to that conviction. Dad was my father, ergo he must be an adult. Only married adults had children, which he was and did. He worked every weekday instead of attending school, the province of children. Teachers, it's true, were adults, but they were also all female, i.e., that time period's corps of the less-than-adult adults. Likewise, Dad was taller than me, owned a house, stayed up past 8:00 p.m., smoked cigarettes, drank coffee and beer, and, when provoked, spewed four letter words without getting his mouth washed out with soap. All of these signaled to the child I was that Dad was an adult.

I didn't realize that my father was a little boy in a grown man's body, and one who believed he had been sorely deprived. Dad may not have realized either that he was still a little boy in all but his physical form. Despite being a parent himself, he was still waiting for his mother's unconditional love. Since it hadn't been forthcoming and its lack could never be remediated, he had to seek acknowledgement of his lovability elsewhere. And others, even farmers from whom he bought eggs, should have known without being explicitly told that he was worthy of nothing less than everyone's tender esteem.

Children, whom adults beget to provide themselves with a purpose in life as well as a wellspring of unstinting love, they in particular should be ever mindful of that obligation. A fetus should have – must have – incorporated the unmet, unarticulated longings imprinted on its parents' strands of DNA along with the knowledge of how to assuage such neediness. But, somehow, my brothers and I were born deficient in that respect. We stumbled through our childhood under the black cloud of Dad's sour disapproval, forever failing to please him and never recognizing the guideposts to his favor.

Perhaps, he did plod through his adult life of responsibilities troubled by a vague sense that something was amiss. That might explain his testy personality. He was selfish, secretive, and critical – but not self-critical. His subconscious mind might have concluded that, if he could keep the components of his life in order and in balance, his indwelling demons would also remain in a state of equilibrium. But it's impossible for me to put forward anything other than speculations. The only emotion I saw him express, whether by physical posture or gesture, word choice, tone of voice or decibel, was anger. The only information he shared with me in regards to his judgment of me was that I was so irremediably fat, lazy, and stupid that the world would be a better place if I kept my mouth shut and my hands occupied, and he or my husband would do my thinking for me.

<hr />

I was rendered breathless when Mammoo also revealed to me that Dad wet the bed until he was thirteen. My brother, Brad, was a bed-wetter during his childhood and beyond. When I left home at nineteen, Brad was fifteen and probably still wetting the bed. This problem provoked daily drama. Mom complained about the urine-saturated pajamas and sheets but tackled the problem with practical maneuvers. She spread a plastic pad over his bed sheet. Before she herself retired for the night, she pulled Brad out of his bed and walked him to the toilet. Except for a glass of milk with his supper, he was not allowed to drink any liquids after 3:00 p.m. Dad addressed the problem by swearing at Brad, threatening to punish him, and publicly ridiculing him. So I was astounded to learn that Dad had been a bed-wetter himself. Having experienced that humiliation himself, how could he treat Brad so cruelly?

Decades later, I knew the answer to that and many similar questions. I understood that Dad acted as he did for the same reason Mom conferred preferential treatment upon David. They were just following the pattern. Their parents had managed these issues in a certain manner, so, when they themselves became parents, Mom and Dad gave it no further thought and adhered to the formula their parents had employed. For whatever reason, they didn't use their pain and hunger for love as a lesson that they needed to seek an alternate path.

Don't assume that I came to this understanding in one insightful flash. I spent years of my adult life in therapy working to exorcise the demons with which my parents infected me. And I spent even longer preparing my mind for introspection by means of the spiritual disciplines of yoga and meditation. These practices invite self-examination. And examining myself enabled me to realize the commonality of all sentient beings. All sentient beings, and that perforce must include my parents, want to be happy, but all of us are beset by an ignorance that induces us to believe that our own happiness must be gained by thwarting the happiness of others. Certainly, if Dad was unhappy, he endeavored to make everyone surrounding him unhappy, too. Mom sprang after every little pleasure and sought to avoid misery. But she did so, initially frequently and later always, by means of Johnnie Walker liquid pain medication. They both died in their mid-fifties before they could alter the manner in which they lived.

I was fortunate, but they weren't. I received – or created – opportunities to become aware that I was on a journey towards a state of no preferences. Heaven, Nirvana, Samadhi – however you wish to characterize it – is easy to attain for the one who has no preferences. It is not a problem to travel the most difficult path necessary to reach that perfect goal if you don't prefer the easy path. For most of us, including myself, though, the journey is the goal because we are fallible human beings. We were born with a human consciousness and the potential for perceiving that we are on a journey in search of our transcendent moment of union with the divine. We already have as much of the gift of heaven as we can presently manage.

28

The Black Camel Kneels at Our Gate

THE FIERY DEMISE of the poultry house marked the beginning of the end. Those destroying and tempering flames tipped me into a cascade of events whose stopping point I couldn't envision.

I was sleeping over at my best friend Karen's house that fateful evening. Her older twin sisters, Judy and Linda, gave up their bedroom and its twin beds at the front of the house for us. Karen and I were already in those beds under the covers when we heard the fire engine's siren.

Today, my husband and I live in a high rise at the intersection of two of Chicago's main thoroughfares within walking distance of a fire station; on the ambulance route to three hospitals; kitty-corner from the largest single-room occupancy, supportive-housing facility in the Midwest (according to its website ymcachicago.org/pages/lawson-house-ymca); and one block from both a McDonald's known in the hood as the crack Donald's, and the Chicago Transit Authority's self-described most dangerous stop on its north-south electric railcar line. If we hear fire truck, ambulance, or police sirens, well, they're so integral to our environment that our ears hear them,

241

and our brains identify the sound without attachment. It's literally in one ear and out the other without detours. And so much mayhem transpires within any twenty-four hours in the city that every form of modern media available to us neglects reporting most of it. The result being that, even if we should take note of alarms in the night, the sounds remain uncoupled from any significance because we seldom learn what triggered the distress signal.

But in Marshall fifty years ago, with its one main street, one traffic light, and a fire department which operated out of a two truck garage attached to City Hall and composed of paid volunteers, that siren wailing in the dark of night meant something out of the ordinary was unfolding. Karen and I dropped into equally dark sleep, however, not knowing what was astir. Mr. Kannemacher, Karen's father, woke us early the next morning to make this report, "There was a fire at the poultry house last night." He hadn't wanted to alarm me by telling us the night before. He was a lanky man. I remember him leaning, like a slightly darker slash of beige, against the eggshell white bedroom wall. I can't quite recall, but he may have also informed us – but most specifically me – that no one was injured. The poultry house building, however, was destroyed. I heard what he said but didn't comprehend the implications of what he was telling me. I didn't know yet how this event was about to change the course of my life.

The fire began in the evening after everyone had left the poultry house but not so late that all good people were already abed, thereby leaving Archer Avenue and the Courthouse Square deserted. A chance passer-by noticed flames or smoke, initiating a linked chain of fortunate coincidences. It was happenstance that Uncle Lauf was in one of the bars along Archer Avenue that evening. I don't recall which bar, but does that matter? It was happenstance also that someone knew he was there and carried the awful news to him, and fortunate coincidence again that he had his business keys in his pocket. With several or all of the able-bodied patrons in the bar that night, Uncle Lauf rushed over to the poultry house. The scale of Marshall's main business area would have put them within a mere one to three blocks of the burning building.

The flatbed truck Uncle Lauf and Dad used for their business was backed into the delivery dock, fully loaded with wood slat coops stuffed with white leghorn hens destined for early morning delivery to Chicago's Water Street market. That was another fortunate coincidence. I can imagine the squawking cacophony broadcast by the panicky fowl. That is, if the smoke hadn't overcome them, but I didn't hear that it had. Uncle Lauf was able to drive the truck out of the building and park it further down the street. Six men lifted the egg-grading machine onto their shoulders and walked it out of the crackling building.

Those few incidents are what rise up from memories of adult conversations overheard fifty years ago. What I don't remember hearing is what caused the fire, if indeed that was ever determined. If I ever heard who noticed flames or smoke in or issuing from the building and alerted Uncle Lauf, those facts have also evaporated from my memory. The day after the fire, I ventured over to the site where the poultry house had withstood decades as the sentinel of that corner. Whether I went alone or, most likely, with David or other family or friends is also beyond recall.

Except for a few charred boards still stubbornly upright, the greater expanse of the perimeter walls wearing their layers of paint and decay had swooned inward pulling the roof, like a blanket, down over themselves. The fallen building, now a yard tall assemblage of debris, emitted occasional spirals of ash or smoke when disturbed by anyone seeking whatever could be salvaged. But mostly all that I can conjure forth of the remains of the poultry house is a vague sense of a crumbly dull gap roofed over by the blue vault of heaven, which had replaced the stamped tin ceiling of the formerly imposing archaic storefront.

During the weeks that followed I parroted the comments of the adults huddled within hearing range, "Yes, it was fortunate that the truck and egg grader were saved but so many smaller but necessary items like tarps and ropes that would be cumulatively expensive to replace had been lost. And how would they replace the building?" I didn't know what I was talking about. I wanted to appear knowledgeable and be included in the circles of nervous conversation.

Uncle Lauf elected to continue the enterprise he had inherited from his father Pop, operating it out of his garage. I remember the egg crates, which previously aggregated in the cooler side room of the poultry house, began stacking up where a second car would have been parked. According to 1989 funeral home records, Uncle Lauf owned and operated his poultry business for an additional eighteen years. The onrush of progress in agricultural production and distribution probably doomed Uncle Lauf's local, small-scale poultry and egg business. Sometime after 1976, he ended thirty years in that business to become a safety inspector for the State of Illinois.

As to my father, I don't know what the story was there. No adult, not even my parents, would have considered that topic any of my business anyway. So I didn't know then and still don't whether there were insufficient prospects for Dad to be included as Uncle

Lauf attempted to rebuild the family business or whether Dad had lost heart or lost interest. Or another likely possibility, Mom badgered Dad into returning to Chicago, where they had originally met. Chicago offered both more certain employment possibilities as well as a helping hand from Mammoo and Pappoo.

Within months, Dad was working in Chicago during the week – I don't even know where or doing what – and living in the second bedroom of Mammoo and Pappoo's apartment. After his Friday shift ended, he drove back to Marshall to spend the weekend with us. Behind his castle walls again, Dad made fun of the sandwiches Mammoo made for his lunch pail and all the little bowls, each containing a few tablespoons of vegetables, with which she encircled Pappoo's supper plate. Meanwhile, I walked around with a quiet smile on my face as if I were happy to have him home again. Dad and I never had much to say to each other previously, and our altered living arrangements didn't provide any new avenues of conversation. Sunday evening he drove back to Chicago. Mom, my brothers and I settled in for another four and a half days free of the miasma of anger he radiated and the fear and tension he provoked. It couldn't last, of course. The age of semi-permanent long-distance commutes that separated family members belonged to a future other than ours.

We moved from the old Montgomery house in farm country to the two bedrooms, kitchen and living room carved out of the Sineni family's basement in Chicago's Roseland neighborhood. We also had access to a bathtub, toilet, and two laundry sinks, instead of a bathroom sink, behind their basement furnace. Its combined square footage was probably about equal to that of our former brooder house and hen yard. Someone had to explain to me why there were bars on the windows and the necessity for both the front and back door to be locked at all times. The window curtains were usually pulled shut to obstruct the appraising stares of passing strangers. And everyone who passed by was a stranger.

My brothers and I were repeatedly ordered not to step off the sidewalks. Marshall residents had yards; Chicagoans possessed lawns manicured for visual appeal, not for children to tread upon. Even the Sineni's backyard was off limits to our games. The only concession was that our mother was allowed to hang her laundry on the clotheslines crisscrossing that space. One day she filled the clotheslines with her week's worth of laundered bed sheets and children's garments in the morning and came out in the afternoon to collect them only to find the entire backyard buried in a foot-deep layer of fertilizer impregnated with horse manure. Her freshly washed laundry was saturated with the odor of it. Since this wasn't Marshall, no one had knocked on the door of her basement apartment or jumped on the phone to warn her that her sheets, towels, and children's' clothes were hanging in the way of hard-working yardmen trying to do their job, and she should do something about that situation. Nor was it a simple matter for her to throw back into a washing machine what was now more foully soiled than her husband and five children could have achieved. We owned only an old Maytag wringer washer. Her fall back option was to haul the stinking mess and her five offspring ranging in age from newborn to a sullen fourteen year old several miles to Mammoo and Pappoo's home to utilize their old Maytag wringer washer and the clothes lines strung back and forth across their backyard between their three-flat building and their garage.

Living cheek to cheek in the Sineni's basement reaffirmed that, in fact, we didn't enjoy each other's company. In the old Montgomery house on our fourteen acres we had been able to avoid acknowledging that sentiment as adeptly as we had avoided being together in the same places at the same times. I missed the expansive physical space available to me in Marshall. It had been pleasant for each of us to have a separate area about the house or land to work or hide in. But, more than anything, I missed being connected to the encircling physical world. My husband doesn't understand such a feeling because he wasn't raised in such close contact with and dependence upon the land. He grew up in traditional suburbs where the environment outside the house was bleak and stifling and served only as a transit medium between indoor spaces.

His growing up in such a milieu forestalled his ability to form the pre-conscious attachment I developed in Marshall to the ground upon which I stood. He lacks the primal happiness and the understanding of it that I experience in seeing the fecund sable earth of the prairie, the green and the golden profusion of the crops and grasses and forbs erupting from it, the shy and sly feral animals that traverse it. My husband's family didn't search day to day for signs favorable or ominous to be revealed by the overarching daytime sky that exhibited every variation of the color blue in the artist's palette, and its sooty nightside twin pricked by astral bodies. Unlike the residents of Marshall, neither he nor his family stood sentinel upon their metaphorical watchtowers to await the wind that either blows down upon you or holds at bay the nurturing rains of life and prosperity; and carries smells as welcome as the petrichor released by the water-soaked soil or as offensive as

Velsicol's pernicious fumes; the so faint nasal tickle from blossomy prairie rose and lilies-of-the-valley perfumeries; the ripe odors of the livestock and their cow chips and horse apples, or the high summer stench of a barrow's fly-blown carcass like a gravy spoon jabbed against the back of your throat. My husband and his family did not attend to the everlasting hymn raised to the golden orb of life by crows and chickens, quietly clattering quacking aspen leaves, and all else that beat their tattoo upon the land or are rooted in the earth and overseen by Sol. Nor were his people chanted into sleep by the cooing pigeons backed up by their ensemble of thrumming and droning cicadas, crickets, and grasshoppers reinforced by the basso profundo of bullfrogs. They did not hover with fond concern over their herds and flocks, their orchards, pastures, and sown fields as God supposedly does over his creatures, and mothers over the children they carried under their hearts for nine months. But we in Marshall did. And all that percolated through my green and tender sprouting self to take up residence within my anima. I thought I lived on land my father owned, but I was deceived. The land owns me, and divorce is impossible.

I'm sure my husband's family home featured a picture window, but it didn't serve as an eye on the world, rather it was the focusing apparatus of the panopticon. The picture in the window wasn't the outdoors; it was the people and their possessions within, cynosure for the passing spectators. The rows of windows in the old Montgomery house were of a width equal to the doors, nearly as tall as the walls in which they were mounted, and they shimmied in their frames when tapped by the constant prairie wind. They had been installed one hundred years prior to admit the light and the sights of the outer world into the inner spaces of the sheltering home. The home's inhabitants and furnishings were not the world's show. People and events passing by were the menagerie.

My husband and I paused at Blizzard Ford on a July 2013 trip to Marshall. He pulled our rental car off the interstate onto the gravel of Blizzard Road, and scrambled down the embankment with me to reach the ford. He did it to please me. I did it to enter again the communion of earth and water; sun and sky; bird, beast, and flower; and all they embrace. People have passed to their eternal reward, buildings collapsed, a way of life has decayed and dissolved back into the spiritus mundi, but the land undergirds each present moment and the memory of what is seen no more.

Over my head, luminous cumulus clouds, their underbellies and trailing edges blue-gray, were suspended in the dome of heaven. At my feet stood that mutable line of convergence where the sheet of water ran over the sandstone shelf at that moment. From there, I watched the current hurry east under the bridge in the course of its own mystic journey. The flowing water was biscuit brown except where irregularities in the shallowest stretches of the sandstone streambed impeded its surging rush forward, creating clusters of argent uplifts. It looked to be possible to wade across the ford to the opposite bank in those areas. A few fingerling fish steadied themselves in pockets of the current that were of a hand's depth. But prior to the shallows I observed an elliptical patch of unruffled dark umber where I couldn't see fish or sandstone whorls or anything beneath its opaque veneer.

Muddy depressions along the stream's edge evidenced recent rising and receding water levels. Wild plants had taken root sparsely within fractures of the sedimentary rock that extended out from under the slope rising up to Blizzard Road, and which was probably least often submerged. Predatory long-bodied dragonflies with their double set of strong transparent wings and their slender relatives the jewel-toned damselflies flitted silently about this vegetation questing for small prey.

The radiant sun pressed warm rays against my exposed back. Unless I leaned into the few and small wild flowers tucked here and there on straggly stalks or in low-lying clumps of sage green shrubbery, that same sun blanched out their slight odor. The water of the ford gurgled as it purled along its route over the uneven surface of its sandstone bed. Unseen cicadas, crickets, and grasshoppers droned in ascending and descending symphonic movements, lapsing at intervals into soundless intermissions.

And I was suspended between the outbreath and the inbreath of the universe in *pratyahara,* the consciousness that beholds the Self in all things according to the fifteen-fold path described in the sacred Indian text: *Tejo-Bindu-Upanishad.*

Bibliography

Berry, Wendell. *The Hidden Wound.* San Francisco: Northpoint Press, 1989.

Budrys, Algis. *Who?.* New York: Ballantine Books, 1975.

Coontz, Stephanie. *The Way We Never Were: American Families and the Nostalgia Trap.* New York: Basic Books, 1992.

Creadick, Anna G. *Perfectly Average: The Pursuit of Normality in Postwar America.* Amherst and Boston: University of Massachusetts Press, 2010.

Gilbert, James Burkhart. *Men in the Middle: Searching for Masculinity in the 1950s.* Chicago: The University of Chicago Press, 2005.

Halberstam, David. *The Fifties.* New York: Ballantine Books, 1994.

Haralovich, Mary Beth. "Sitcoms and Suburbs: Positioning the 1950s Homemaker," in *Private Screenings: Television and the Female Consumer*, eds. Lynn Spiegel and Denise Mann. Minneapolis: University of Minnesota Press, 1992.

Hendrick, George, ed. *To Reach Eternity: The Letters of James Jones.* With a foreward by William Styron. New York: Random House, 1989.

Hendrick, George, Helen Howe and Don Sackrider. *James Jones and the Handy Writers' Colony.* Carbondale and Edwardsville, IL: Southern Illinois University Press, 2001.

Jeffords, Michael, Susan L. Post and Kenneth R. Robertson. *Illinois Wilds.* Urbana, IL: Phoenix Publishing, 1995.

Legacy Publishing, Div. of Publications International, Ltd. *The Fifties Chronicle.* With a foreward by Margaret Truman. Consultants:

Beth Bailey, Ph.D. and David Farber, Ph.D. Lincolnwood, IL: Publications International, Ltd., 2006.

MacShane, Frank. *Into Eternity: The Life of James Jones, American Writer.* Boston: Houghton Mifflin Co., 1985.

Olausen, Judy. *Mother.* With an introduction by Karin Winegar. New York: Penguin Studio Books, 1996.

Schwartz, Robert. *Your Soul's Plan: Discovering the Real Meaning of the Life You Planned Before You Were Born.* Previously published as *Courageous Souls: Do We Plan Our Life Challenges Before Birth?* Berkeley, CA: Frog Books, an Imprint of North Atlantic Books, 2007, 2009.

Ibid. Your Soul's Gift: The Healing Power of the Life You Planned Before You Were Born. Chesterland, OH: Whispering Winds Press, 2012.

Yenne, Bill. *Going Home to the Fifties.* San Francisco: Last Gasp of San Francisco, 2002.

About the Author

Judith Forsythe wrote this memoir to, as she explained, "reveal that not all of us born in the forties and fifties lived in families and circumstances as idealized in the family sitcoms of the fifties, and that farms were family farms, not factories."

Her future writing projects include a collection of short stories (*The Accidental Mother*), a three-part autobiographical fiction novel (*The Sieve of Morpheus*) and a collection of poetry (*Generated by Time and Circumstance*).

Judith was born in 1944 in Chicago, where she currently resides with her husband of thirty-two years and two shelter rescue cats. She received a BA degree in English Literature and MS degree in Library and Information Sciences, both from the University of Illinois.

Receive a FREE chapter of Judith Forsythe's next book of short stories by visiting www.JudithForsythe.com/bonus

Connect with Judith directly at Judith@JudithForsythe.com

www.ingramcontent.com/pod-product-compliance
Lightning Source LLC
LaVergne TN
LVHW051501080426
835509LV00017B/1859